Mediating Literary Borders: Asian Australian Writing

Engaging with Asian Australian writing, this book focuses on an influential area of cultural production defined by its ethnic diversity and stylistic innovativeness, Asian Australian writing. In addressing the demanding new transnational and transcultural critical frameworks of such syncretic writing, the contributors collectively examine how the varied and diverse body of Asian Australian literary work intervenes into contemporary representational politics and culture. The book questions, for instance, the ideology of Australian multiculturalism; the core/periphery hierarchy; the perpetuation of Orientalist attitudes and stereotypes; and white Australian claims to belong as seen in its myths of cultural authenticity and authority. Ranging in critical analyses from the historic first Chinese-Australian novel to contemporary award winning Sri Lankan, Bangladeshi and Filipino Australian novels, the book provides an inside view of the ways in which Asian Australian literary work is reshaping Australian mainstream literature, politics and culture, and in the wider context, the world literary scene.

This book was originally published as a special issue of the *Journal of Postcolonial Writing*.

Janet Wilson is Professor of English and Postcolonial Studies at the University of Northampton, UK. She has published widely on Australian and New Zealand postcolonial and diaspora writing and cinema, including guest-edited journals and essay collections, recently *The Routledge Diaspora Studies Reader*. She co-edits the series, Studies in World Literature, and the *Journal of Postcolonial Writing*.

Chandani Lokugé is Associate Professor of Literary Studies at Monash University, Australia. Among her 15 book publications are the Oxford Classics Reissues series of Indian women's writing, three novels and several guest-edited journals, including the *Journal of Postcolonial Writing*. She edited the *Annotated Bibliography of English Studies* for Routledge from 2007–2009.

T0347519

Mediating Literary Borders: Asian Australian Writing

Edited by
Janet Wilson and Chandani Lokugé

Routledge
Taylor & Francis Group

LONDON AND NEW YORK

First published 2018 by Routledge

2 Park Square, Milton Park, Abingdon, Oxfordshire OX14 4RN
52 Vanderbilt Avenue, New York, NY 10017

Routledge is an imprint of the Taylor & Francis Group, an informa business

First issued in paperback 2019

British Library Cataloguing in Publication Data
A catalogue record for this book is available from the British Library

ISBN 13: 978-1-138-57081-8 (hbk)
ISBN 13: 978-0-367-89249-4 (pbk)

Typeset in Minion Pro
by RefineCatch Limited, Bungay, Suffolk

Publisher's Note
The publisher accepts responsibility for any inconsistencies that may have arisen during the conversion of this book from journal articles to book chapters, namely the possible inclusion of journal terminology.

Disclaimer
Every effort has been made to contact copyright holders for their permission to reprint material in this book. The publishers would be grateful to hear from any copyright holder who is not here acknowledged and will undertake to rectify any errors or omissions in future editions of this book.

Contents

Citation Information

The chapters in this book were originally published in the *Journal of Postcolonial Writing*, volume 52, issue 5 (October 2016). When citing this material, please use the original page numbering for each article, as follows:

Introduction
    Realigning the margins: Asian Australian writing
    Janet Wilson and Chandani Lokugé
    Journal of Postcolonial Writing, volume 52, issue 5 (October 2016), pp. 527–532

Chapter 1
    Poison, polygamy and postcolonial politics: The first Chinese Australian novel
    Zhong Huang and Wenche Ommundsen
    Journal of Postcolonial Writing, volume 52, issue 5 (October 2016), pp. 533–544

Chapter 2
    (Not) being at home: Hsu Ming Teo's Behind the Moon *(2005) and Michelle de Kretser's* Questions of Travel *(2012)*
    Janet Wilson
    Journal of Postcolonial Writing, volume 52, issue 5 (October 2016), pp. 545–558

Chapter 3
    Mediating literary borders: Sri Lankan writing in Australia
    Chandani Lokugé
    Journal of Postcolonial Writing, volume 52, issue 5 (October 2016), pp. 559–571

Chapter 4
    Tourists, travellers, refugees: An interview with Michelle De Kretser
    Alexandra Watkins
    Journal of Postcolonial Writing, volume 52, issue 5 (October 2016), pp. 572–580

Chapter 5
    The diasporic slide: representations of second-generation diasporas in Yasmine Gooneratne's A Change of Skies *(1991) and in Chandani Lokugé's* If the Moon Smiled *(2000) and* Softly as I Leave You *(2011)*
    Alexandra Watkins
    Journal of Postcolonial Writing, volume 52, issue 5 (October 2016), pp. 581–594

Chapter 6

"The root of all evil"? Transnational cosmopolitanism in the fiction of Dewi Anggraeni, Simone Lazaroo and Merlinda Bobis
Paul Giffard-Foret
Journal of Postcolonial Writing, volume 52, issue 5 (October 2016), pp. 595–609

Chapter 7

Merlinda Bobis's Fish-Hair Woman: *Showcasing Asian Australianness, putting the question of justice in its place*
Dolores Herrero
Journal of Postcolonial Writing, volume 52, issue 5 (October 2016), pp. 610–621

Chapter 8

Re-storying the past, re-imagining the future in Adib Khan's Homecoming *and* Spiral Road
Stefano Mercanti
Journal of Postcolonial Writing, volume 52, issue 5 (October 2016), pp. 622–633

For any permission-related enquiries please visit:
http://www.tandfonline.com/page/help/permissions

Notes on Contributors

Paul Giffard-Foret is a sessional Lecturer at the Sorbonne in Paris, France. His research is concerned with postcolonial critical theory, Asian Australian studies, diasporic and multi-cultural literatures.

Dolores Herrero is accredited Full Professor of English Literature at the Department of English and German Philology at the University of Zaragoza, Spain. Her main interests are postcolonial literature and cinema, on which she has published extensively.

Zhong Huang is Associate Professor in English Literatures and Director of the Australian Studies Centre at Wuhan University, China. He is the editor of the journal *Australian Cultural Studies*, and has published articles in a number of journals, including *Journal of the Association for the Study of Australian Literature* (*JASAL*) and *Antipodes*.

Chandani Lokugé is Associate Professor of Literary Studies at Monash University, Australia. Among her 15 book publications are the Oxford Classics Reissues series of Indian women's writing, three novels and several guest-edited journals, including the *Journal of Postcolonial Writing*. She edited the *Annotated Bibliography of English Studies for Routledge* from 2007–2009.

Stefano Mercanti is a Research Fellow at the University of Udine, Italy, where he is also a member of the Partnership Studies Group (PSG), and associate editor of the online journal on modern literatures, *Le Simplegadi*. He has published widely on postcolonial literature and partnership studies.

Wenche Ommundsen is Research Professor of English Literatures at the University of Wollongong, Australia, where she was Dean of the Faculty of Arts from 2009 to 2013. Most of her recent work has had a particular focus on Asian Australian writing. Current research projects include an Australian Research Council-funded study of Australian literature in languages other than English.

Alexandra Watkins teaches Literary Studies at Deakin University, Australia, where she also completed her PhD. Her research interests include postcolonial fiction, South Asian diaspora fiction, Australian multiculturalism policy, Islamophobia, touristic literatures, new media and genre studies.

Janet Wilson is Professor of English and Postcolonial Studies at the University of Northampton, UK. She has published widely on Australian and New Zealand postcolonial and diaspora writing and cinema, including guest-edited journals and essay collections, recently *The Routledge Diaspora Studies Reader*. She co-edits the series, Studies in World Literature, and the *Journal of Postcolonial Writing*.

Introduction: Realigning the margins: Asian Australian writing

Janet Wilson and Chandani Lokugé

This special issue of the *Journal of Postcolonial Writing*, the result of a collaboration with the South Asian Diaspora International Research Network (SADIRN) at Monash University, Australia, engages with Asian Australian writing, a phenomenon that has been staking out a place in the Australian literary landscape since the 1950s and 1960s. It has now burgeoned into an influential area of cultural production, known for its ethnic diversity and stylistic innovativeness, and demanding new forms of critical engagement involving transnational and transcultural frameworks. As Wenche Ommundsen and Huang Zhong point out in their article in this issue, the very term "Asian Australian" signals a heterogeneity that rivals that of the dominant Anglo Australian culture; just as white Australian writing displays the lineaments of its complex European heritage, so hybridized works by multicultural writers from mainland China, Vietnam, Hong Kong, the Philippines, Indonesia, India, Pakistan, Sri Lanka, Cambodia, Singapore and Malaysia can be read in terms of their specific national, ethnic, linguistic and cultural traditions. Nevertheless, this category's primary location within the space of the host or Australian nation has determined its reception and interpretation. Marked by controversial representations of historical and present-day encounters with white Australian culture, and debates on alterity representational inequality, and conscious of its minority status, Asian Australian writing has become a force field of critical enquiry in its own right (Ommundsen 2012, 2).

Collectively the seven articles and one interview in this special issue examine how this varied and culturally diverse body of work intervenes into contemporary representational politics: for example, in questioning the ideology of Australian multiculturalism, the core/periphery hierarchy, the perpetuation of Orientalist attitudes and stereotypes, and white Australian claims to belong as seen in its myths of cultural authenticity and authority. Ameliorative multicultural discourses are also identified, reflecting fiction's power to imagine more positive realms of potentiality and healing: Chandani Lokugé claims that Sri Lankan Australian fiction assumes an intermediary role in developing "intercultural conversations in Australia as a conduit into national harmony"; Dolores Herrero argues that the novel *Fish-Hair Woman* by Filipino writer Merlinda Bobis, whose heroine's monstrous hair "encodes the melodrama of transnational subjectivity", opens up space for a "transformative dialogue" that might compensate for the violence and trauma of the colonial past; while Stefano Mercanti identifies a reconciliatory mode in novels by the Australian

Bangladeshi writer Adib Khan, whereby diversity is seen as enriching cross-cultural dialogue and fostering interaction. Articles by Janet Wilson and Paul Giffard-Foret identify
the hopeful formation of alternative communities – for example, of vulnerable migrants or
children of migrants linked by ties of affection and empathy – in Hsui Ming Teo's *Behind
the Moon* and Merlinda Bobis's novel *The Solemn Lantern Maker*. Yet tensions due to issues
of official entry, visas, citizenship and limited acceptance of the Asian subject by the Anglo
Celtic majority also persist. Alongside the strict controls on immigration into Australia,
the branding of refugees as illegal, and the struggle to gain citizenship, are other signs
of subtle discrimination: the misinterpretations and misappellations of the cross-cultural
encounter, subject of Yasmine Gooneratne's seminal novel *A Change of Skies* (1991), and
a continued "masked racism" – nuanced forms of stereotyping by which Asian migrants
and their descendants are exoticized and "othered" (Ang 2001, 146). Informing the critical
positioning of most articles here is the problematic history of Asian Australian relations
that can be traced to the White Australia policy of 1901 in which Asia was demonized as
Australia's "utterly distrusted Other" (Huggan 2007, 131, citing Ang 2001, 130), while also
representing its "most fertile imaginative territory" (Huggan 2007, 132); as Herrero points
out, even today Australia's self-location outside Asia comes from having "no deep affinity
for the region". The current upsurge in Asian Australian writing, as well as the critical
discourse which flows from it, can therefore be seen as an attempt to overturn and rewrite
this damning legacy.

Recent novels by writers like Alice Pung, Hsu Ming Teo, Simone Lazaroo, Merlinda
Bobis, Chandani Lokugé, Adib Khan and Michelle de Kretser develop the cross-cultural
approach implied by the compound "Asian Australian", by creating temporal and spatial
complexity and new kinds of subjectivity and community through transnational and historical perspectives. They draw attention to the ongoing plight of new communities exiled
due to the political upheavals that erupted in many Asian nations throughout the second
half of the 20th century, conflicts and disasters which provide historical contexts to narratives of suffering and hardship: the civil war between the Government and Liberation
Tigers of Tamil Eelam (LTTE) in Sri Lanka (Michelle de Krester's novel *Questions of Travel*
and Chandani Lokugé's novel, *Softly, as I Leave You*), the ravages of the Vietnam War and
the Australian and US presence in Vietnam (Adib Khan's *Homecoming* and Tsui Ming Teo's
Behind the Moon); the US control of the Philippines, the Total War of President Marcos in
the Philippines of 1987–89 against communist insurgency, and the post-9/11 US-led global
War on Terror (Merlinda Bobis's *The Fish-Hair Woman* and *The Solemn Lantern Maker*).
Such writing points to the layered, intersecting genealogies of global diasporas, and issues
that are specific to the Asian Australian context can be mapped onto universal themes that
emerge in representations of the fate of migrant, refugee communities, poverty, religious
fundamentalism, trauma, inequality, racial discrimination. These underpin stories of chance
survival, quests for new opportunities, and questions about belonging in the lives of professionals, migrants, and asylum seekers who arrive at an alien society and into radically
different circumstances, and whose descendants seek to adjust to their inherited problems
of location and their tangled genealogies.

Asian Australian writing also takes its place on the stage of world literature due to its
persistent focus on the dilemma of the exile and outsider, ranging from the diasporic double
consciousness to a more universal, existential angst. It can be read as transnational, globalized writing, like other fiction about populations displaced from nations like Lebanon,

Egypt and India. Questions of how to create home in diaspora and discover new ways of belonging for the dislocated subject who is affected by memory, trauma and distance as well as the unpredictability of the new are common to all diaspora writings. Representations of migrant liminality, of the predicament of being "neither here nor there", of inhabiting "a third space" (Madsen 2006, 120), are constructed round questions about home and homeland return. For the second generation these issues take a different form as Alexandra Watkins discusses in her article: the children of migrants may reduplicate the ambiguous sense of belonging of their parents through their negotiations between two cultures, or more dramatically fail to live up to the expectations of the first generation. Yet both migrants and their descendants share a "homing desire", and engage with new identifying practices by which to reinvent home in the diaspora (Brah 1996, 180). These can include return visits to the country of origin, driven by nostalgia and longing, and the wish to reconnect, renew and sustain cultural and ancestral roots, as Stefano Mercanti's study of Adib Khan's novels *Seasonal Adjustments* (1994) and *Spiral Road* (2007) shows. Khan's protagonists who return from Australia to Bangladesh have to renegotiate the relationship with the past, and gain a more distanced perspective on both worlds, while for the elite cosmopolitan heroine of Dewi Anggraeni's novel *The Root of All Evil*, who returns to her original homeland of Jakarta, the shock comes from a miscalculation, as Paul Giffard-Foret points out, that her well-intended hospitality would improve the material circumstances of subaltern women. Both Giffard-Foret and Dolores Hererro situate "Australia in Asia", examining the plight of white Australian travellers and displaced citizens in the transplanted settings and cosmopolitan frames of recent novels: the war-torn zone of the Philippines in Merlinda Bobis's *The Fish-Hair Woman* and *The Solemn Lantern Maker*, and the neocolonial touristic setting of paradisal Bali in Simone Lazaroo's *Sustenance*. Michelle de Kretser, by contrast, in her global novel *Questions of Travel* depicts the multiple foreign destinations of her vulnerable, globe-trotting Australian heroine, but omits any reference to the Australian presence in the parallel narrative set in Colombo, Sri Lanka. Nevertheless, all such novels, whether set within or outside national borders, confirm that fictions about exile are a way of dealing with the consequences of migration, for as Lee (2016) says, "through embracing the diasporic imaginary the novel tries to find new ways to affirm unbridgeable distances in the world" (133).

The modes of production and diverse readerships that underlie the canon-formation of Chinese Australian writing – the largest of the Asian Australian subgenres – is the subject of Wenche Ommundsen and Huang Zhong's opening article. The Australian Chinese novel, *The Poison of Polygamy*, serialized in the Chinese-language newspaper *The Chinese Times* (Melbourne) in 1909–10, is, the authors claim, the very first Australian Chinese novel, preceding by seven decades the first significant narrative in English about the Chinese in Australia, commonly recognised as Brian Castro's *Birds of Passage* (1983). To compare two such founding moments and seminal works about Asian-Australian relations is to be made more aware of the changes in self-definition, and the growth of ironic self-awareness within the Chinese Australian community and its descendants that Castro's novel demonstrates. The lurid tale of polygamy, murder and sexual betrayal of *The Poison of Polygamy* is interspersed with the narrator's commentary on China's decadence during the Qing Dynasty which drove its citizens into exile: foot-binding, illiteracy, opium addiction and other rebarbative practices are found surviving in rural Australia. The novel's criticism of imperial China is "self-orientalizing" and it perpetuates the same stereotypes of the Chinese by which they were demonized by white Australians. By contrast to the semi-collusion with Anglo Celtic racist prejudice that marks out this critical, reformist, anti-imperial text, Castro's narrator in *Birds of Passage* deliberately defies categories of national and racial identity and is able to "negotiate a space for himself between other people's imprisoning definitions of him" (Huggan 2007, 135).

In her article, Janet Wilson examines the ways in which Asian migrants and their descendants destabilize the core/periphery binary of the multicultural nation by undermining the space of Anglo-Celtic Australians within the nation state. Hsu Ming Teo's youthful characters in *Behind the Moon* undertake practices of not-being-at-home as Teo queers normative Australian categories of identity and belonging in order to address the problems of multiculturalism and expose white Australian vulnerability. The white Australian, Gibbo, one of three young "multicultural rejects", empathetically identifies with Asianness, recognizing "the other" as part of himself – like the Sri Lankan narrator of Channa Wickremesekera's novel *Asylum*, who absorbs the consciousness of an Afghan boy. Michelle de Kretser's novel *Questions of Travel* implies even greater dilution of white Australian homogeneity and belonging. Her Australian global traveller, Laura, who works for a global travel company, lives an unsettled life of travel and tourism, whereas De Krester's other protagonist, the traumatized Sri Lankan, Ravi, a refugee in Australia, grieving for his murdered wife and child and longing to return home, decides to leave, despite being granted permanent residence, to face an uncertain life in his war-torn country.

Chandani Lokugé and Alexandra Watkins identify a challenging new territory in contemporary Asian Australian culture – the identity fluctuations of the second-generation migrant growing up in Australia, as a result of what Watkins calls the "diasporic slide", defined as "the slip of the diaspora from parent to child". As Watkins theorizes, the second-generation migrant treads the tightrope between parental homeland expectations and the bicultural, blended and multicultural identities that they develop from their acceptance of the diversity of culture within which they grow up. While Watkins explores the comic and tragic consequences of the "diasporic slide" in Yasmine Gooneratne's *A Change of Skies* and Chandani Lokugé's *Softly, as I Leave You* and *If the Moon Smiled*, Lokugé investigates the fluidity with which the second-generation migrant crosses cultural borders into cosmopolitanism in Channa Wickremesekera's novels *Asylum* and *Tracks*. Lokugé also discusses Michelle de Kretser's novel *Questions of Travel* and attributes the protagonist Ravi's inability to settle in Australia to the limited acceptance of migrants, the undermining of aspirations to multicultural interconnectedness, and Ravi's educated, middle-class differences from the stereotypical refugee. She sees hope only for the second generation in the novel's dystopian vision. Given the emphasis on De Kretser's acclaimed novel in the articles by the co-editors of this issue, it is particularly appropriate that we have been able to include an interview with Michelle de Kretser herself, conducted by Alexandra Watkins. Watkins focuses on *Questions of Travel*, and De Kretser discusses issues such as Ravi's character, the political crisis in Sri Lanka which forced her family to leave for Australia in 1972, and the treatment of Sri Lankan migrants in Australia.

Dolores Herrero and Paul Giffard-Foret both turn to the works of Filipino novelist Merlinda Bobis in examining stories that subvert the commonplace Asian-Australian-Asian migrant narrative by using overseas settings. Herrero argues that in her novel *Fish-Hair Woman*, Bobis aims to reconstruct and overturn the painful past of those who disappeared in Marcos's Total War in the Philippines. Her experimental fiction superimposes a realist narrative about the history of oppression in the Philippines on a magical realist one in which multiple stories of the silenced voices of those raped and tortured by Marcos's private army reappear as a way of overcoming the constraints of history, death and trauma. In her "palimpsestuous reading", Herrero shows Bobis challenging the "causal paradigm" of history by drawing attention to "the play of domination". The heroine's multiple storytelling, symbolized by the waving tentacles of her hair, opens up to others' trauma, allowing her "to represent what ultimately transcends the limits of representation", lay the question of justice to rest, and enable cross-cultural understanding and possible new forms of community.

Giffard-Foret claims that top-down strategies of hospitality and forms of transnational cosmopolitanism are seen to fail in novels by East-Asian Australian women writers. Using the model of grass-roots cosmopolitanism and "subaltern hospitality", he traces a bottom-top structure, via "a ladder of privilege. In Simone Lazaroo's novel *Sustenance*, about the neocolonial tourist industry, Australian tourist elites at first control the behaviour of the Balinese villagers, but when terrorists enter the resort hotel and the guests become hostages, "subaltern cosmopolitanism in the form of local hospitality and cuisine emerges". In Bobis's *The Solemn Lantern Maker*, Giffard-Foret finds a similar "wretched cosmopolitanism" in the mutual bonding between four people, two of them children, who come together after accusations of kidnapping an American tourist lead to threats against them when the Filipino government proposes to bulldoze their slum in Manila. Cosmopolitanism, he concludes, is only likely to bring about a more just and democratic society when it is "subaltern" – that is, anchored in communities of women from poor countries.

The question of Asian Australian writing's marginality in relation to the national canon continues to be raised; for example, Herrero notes that Bobis's novel, being set in the Philippines, was at first rejected by Australian publishers. These problems are reminiscent of anglophone Asian diaspora writing in multicultural Canada and the USA, where the Asian presence has been both more pervasive and long-lived, but equally slow to find a distinctive voice and establish a presence. Nevertheless, questions about the canon point to other forms of exclusion or dislocation that this type of writing displays: marginality in the cross-cultural encounter, difference and discrimination, ethnic hybridization, new forms of identity, the search for cultural heritage, the meaning of home and belonging. Like Canadian and American Asian writing, the questions this new literary category raises as it gains purchase in national and global marketplaces, concerning its distinctiveness, raison d'être and national boundaries, are familiar to all emergent minority literatures (Chakraborty 2012). The answers might lie in the field's diversification and continued growth as it challenges the gatekeeping boundaries: the periphery-centre borderline is porous, as developments in the literary landscape of Canada and the USA show, and Asian Australian literature may not be destined to remain a marginal genre, categorized as ethnic/migrant literature. Recently there are signs that it is beginning to reshape the Australian mainstream (it is now taught in schools) and several of the novels under discussion have won national prizes or been highly acclaimed – suggestive of slow acceptance into the canon as its themes and debates become more recognizable and new ways of reading take hold.

Disclosure statement

No potential conflict of interest was reported by the authors.

References

Ang, Ien. 2001. *On Not Speaking Chinese: Living Between Asia and the West*. London: Routledge.

Brah, Avtar. 1996. *Cartographies of Diaspora: Contesting Identities*. London: Routledge.

Chakraborty, Mridula Nath. 2012. "'There Goes the Neighbourhood': The (Indian)-Subcontinental in the Asian/Australian Literary Precinct." *Journal of the Association for the Study of Australian Literature* 12 (2): 1–11. http://openjournals.library.usyd.edu.au/index.php/JASAL/article/view/9814/9702.

Huggan, Graham. 2007. *Australian Literature: Postcolonialism, Racism, Transnationalism*. Oxford: Oxford University Press.

Lee, Yoon Sun. 2016. "The Postcolonial Novel and Diaspora." In *The Cambridge Companion to the Postcolonial Novel*, edited by Ato Quayson, 133–151. Cambridge; Cambridge University Press.

Madsen, Deborah. 2006. "'No Place Like Home': The Ambivalent Rhetoric of Hospitality in the Work of Simone Lazaroo, Arlene Chai and Hsu-Ming Teo." *Journal of Intercultural Studies* 27 (1–2): 117–132.

Ommundsen, Wenche. 2012. "Transnational Imaginaries: Reading Asian Australian Writing." *Journal of the Association for the Study of Australian Literature* 12 (2): 1–8.

Poison, polygamy and postcolonial politics: The first Chinese Australian novel

Zhong Huang and Wenche Ommundsen

ABSTRACT

This article examines the first novel written by a Chinese diaspora writer in Australia, *The Poison of Polygamy* (多妻毒), published in instalments in the Chinese-language newspaper *Chinese Times* (Melbourne) from 1909 to 1910. Set during the Gold Rush of the 1850s, the novel is nevertheless of its own time, reflecting the pressing concerns of a community in turmoil as the political upheavals of China in the final years of the Qing dynasty competed for attention with the disastrous effects of the White Australia policy. Taking the form of a picaresque and cautionary tale warning against traditional practices such as polygamy, opium smoking and foot-binding, the novel seeks to educate members of the lower classes of the Chinese community while embracing the republican cause against the Manchu rulers. The article argues that the progressive political agenda of the text (democratic, feminist) stands in sharp contrast to the view of the Chinese which prevailed in the white Australian community at the time.

When literary scholars in the 1990s "invented" the category "Asian Australian writing" as a subset of Australian multicultural writing (Ommundsen and Boreland 1995), it was not because they knew of a large body of works in need of a new label. The intention, rather, was heuristic, and based on considerable ignorance: from what little we knew about texts by Australian writers with an Asian background, we suspected there was much more we did not know. Inspired by the methods of the pioneers of Australian multicultural literary studies only a decade earlier (Gunew *et al.* 1992; Gunew 1994), we not only wanted to find and document more writers and texts, but beyond that, to discover how writing from these more recent immigrant communities reflected the shift away from Australia's predominantly European cultural traditions that was bound to follow from recent changes in patterns of immigration. The efforts were richly rewarded in the sense that they brought to light established as well as emerging writers and offered scholars a framework for reading texts from various Asian diasporas (also a database).[1] However, possibly the most important discovery was that many previous assumptions about this writing simply did not stand up to scrutiny, and the most problematic of all was the category "Asian Australian writing" itself.

Borrowed from the more established "Asian American" tradition, with its bias towards East Asian diasporas, the term "Asian Australian" struggled from the outset to account for the diversity of national, cultural and linguistic backgrounds it was designed to accommodate. If it still retains some currency today, it is not to suggest any sameness across the category, but on the contrary to signal a heterogeneity not unlike that uncovered by earlier scholars of multicultural literature when they argued that "European" means much more than the dominant Anglo Australian culture (see Gunew 1994). Today, scholars looking to identify trends in Asian diaspora writing are more likely to study particular national/ethnic/cultural traditions (Chinese, Vietnamese, Sri Lankan, etc.), acknowledging that even these categories are far from homogeneous. Thus, while the text to be discussed in this article was, as far as we can establish, the first Asian Australian novel ever to be published, we will read it as an early example of Chinese Australian writing, tracing its specific connections to historical events and cultural debates in China, and in the Chinese community in Australia.

The first Chinese Australian novel, it has for a long time been assumed, was Brian Castro's debut novel *Birds of Passage* (1983), winner of the 1982 Vogel award. In this novel, the early history of Chinese Australia is told through the story of Lo Yun Shan, a gold-digger who along with tens of thousands of his countrymen arrived from Kwantung (Guangdong) province to try his luck in the Victorian goldfields in the 1850s. Juxtaposed with his story is that of Seamus O'Young, an Australian-born Chinese (ABC) born around the same time as the author (1950), and growing up during the final years of the White Australia policy. While historical in parts, the novel is clearly of its own time: race relations on the goldfields are reflected through the lens of a postcolonial and post-White Australia sensibility, and the complex form carries echoes of the movements which inspired experimental fiction emanating from the Americas and Europe in the 1980s: magical realism, postmodernism and post-structuralism (see Brennan 2008).

Brian Castro was not, however, the first Australian of Chinese descent to publish literary fiction. Recent research into the early Chinese Australian press (Kuo 2013) and current work on Chinese-language literary production in Australia[2] have revealed a lively literary scene in the Chinese communities in Sydney and Melbourne around the time of Federation (1901) and pushed back the publication of the first Chinese Australian novel by more than seven decades. Published in instalments in the Melbourne-based Chinese-language newspaper *Chinese Times* between June 1909 and December 1910, an as yet untranslated short novel entitled 多妻毒 (*duo qi du*, in English *The Poison of Polygamy*) entertained readers with the picaresque adventures of its anti-hero Huang Shang-kang while at the same time seeking to educate the lower classes in the Chinese community in the hope of making the community as a whole more acceptable to Australian society. Like *Birds of Passage*, the novel is set during the Gold Rush of the 1850s; also like *Birds of Passage* (albeit without a contemporary narrative strand), it is very much of its own time and place, reflecting the pressing concerns of a community in turmoil as the political upheavals of China in the final years of the Qing dynasty competed for attention with the disastrous effects of the White Australia policy. Formally, it bears witness to its mode of publication through a carefully devised plot development to suit the instalment format; it also caters to its target readership's taste for adventure, intrigue and an unambiguous moral compass.

The aim of this article is to introduce this important but forgotten text to English-speaking readers of Australian and postcolonial literature and to explore its commentary on matters of major concern to the diasporic community at the time of publication. As the novel is yet to be translated into English we will devote considerable space to plot summary and quotation in order to give readers an overview of the story as well as a taste of its narrative voice and its position on issues of debate in the Chinese Australian community. To start with, however, it is necessary to locate the text in its historical moment: a time of crisis from the perspective of which the story of the adventures of Chinese gold-diggers provided both welcome relief and premonitions of the trouble ahead.

At the turn of the 20th century, the Chinese population in Australia was in decline. Restrictions on Chinese immigration, which had been imposed by each separate colonial administration prior to Federation, were soon to be enshrined in the Immigration Restriction Act, or White Australia policy, which was the first piece of legislation to be passed by the Australian parliament in 1901. However, while overall numbers were dwindling, the Chinese population of Sydney and Melbourne was in fact increasing as more Chinese moved to the city to concentrate in certain locations, such as the Rocks in Sydney, and in certain occupations, such as international trade and market gardening. Increasing pressure from anti-Chinese sentiments in the mainstream population galvanized the community and led to calls for greater solidarity, at the same time as political struggles both in China and in the wider Chinese diaspora became issues of major concern. It was in this climate that the first Chinese-language newspapers were launched,[3] the most important of which were the *Chinese Australian Herald* (广益华报 1894) and the *Tung Wah News* (东华新报 1898, after 1902–1936 *Tung Wah Times* 东华报) in Sydney and the *Chinese Times* (1902–1922)[4] in Melbourne. The major issue for debate in the Chinese-language press was the tense political situation in China. While the need for major reform of the corrupt and outdated Qing dynasty was recognized by all, Chinese Australians were divided on how this could best be achieved. The *Tung Wah Times* threw its support behind the Manchu rulers and the Chinese Empire Reform Association, while the *Chinese Times* embraced the revolutionary republican cause. Chinese nationalist sentiment also led to calls for solidarity across the vast Chinese diaspora, among other things taking the shape of a move to boycott American products in protest against the US Chinese Exclusion Act of 1882. Locally, the call for solidarity within the community could not cover up its existing deep divisions and disagreements, not just between monarchists and republicans, but also between the English-speaking Chinese elites and working-class Chinese, between Christians and Confucians, and between the different professions. The elites were in favour of Australia's move towards Federation and keen to emphasize their support for the democratic values underpinning the foundation of the new nation. They were greatly shocked and saddened by the anti-Chinese sentiment and the White Australia policy, but rather than directing their disappointment and anger at white Australians, they tended to blame the lower classes of their own community who in their view damaged the reputation of all Chinese through unacceptable behaviours such as gambling and opium smoking. One of the aims of the Chinese-language newspapers was to discourage some of their traditional practices and thus, through education, strive to make the community more acceptable to white Australian society.

Literary writing became an important tool in this campaign. The *Tung Wah Times* in Sydney was the first to publish literary texts (short stories, poetry and essays) in support of the reform programme.[5] One example is the short story "Horrible Poison", published on December 19, 1908. Set on an Australian sheep farm, it illustrates the deadly effect of opium. A farmer baits beef with opium in order to kill dingos who have been stealing his sheep, but his action has a domino effect: the dingos die after eating the poisoned beef, crows die after feeding on the dead dingos and the sheep eventually die after eating the grass on which the dead crows lie scattered. The reform agenda of the *Tung Wah Times* also included a sharp critique of Confucian patriarchal norms and a push for gender equality. The newspaper published several essays and stories featuring strong female characters and discouraging foot-binding and polygamy. While these texts clearly address issues of relevance to the Chinese in Australia, and in particular to their reputation in the eyes of the wider white Australian community, their social and political agenda was by no means unique to Australia. They were the diasporic expression of a major reform movement which had swept through China in the final decades of the 19th century and which was to have wide-reaching effects. In the political sphere, the toppling of the Qing dynasty in 1911 led to the declaration of the Republic of China; in the cultural and intellectual spheres, it culminated in the May Fourth Movement of 1919, a student demonstration which has been called "The Chinese Renaissance" and which in Chinese revolutionary memory has come to symbolize a break with the old, Confucian tradition and the ushering in of new ideas, inspired by science, democracy and modern, western ways of thinking (see Pan 2015; Mitter 2008). The humiliation of China in modern times, from the colonial wars of the 19th century to the peace deal after World War I, was attributed to the backwardness of the nation's political, social and cultural order. Major reform was needed to bring China into the modern world and redress its international standing. Overseas Chinese were called upon to support different factions of the reform movement, and had their own reasons for doing so, seeing it as their way of counteracting racist stereotypes and gaining greater respect in their host nations. In the period leading up to these events, the diaspora was to play an important role in disseminating the new ideas and in lending support, financial as well as intellectual, to reformers and revolutionaries who were either banned or severely restricted in the homeland.

The Chinese Emperor Reform Association, which was strongly supported by the *Tung Wah Times*, advocated a comprehensive programme of reform and modernization for China, including civic equality, gender equality, racial equality and national equality (see Fitzgerald 2007, 118). Liang Qichao, exiled reformer and prominent spokesman for the Chinese Empire Reform Association, visited Australia from 1900 to 1901. He was one of the most fierce critics of the social, cultural and political order of his home country, and argued for a modernized (and westernized) system which would see China take its place as a proud and equal member of the society of nations. He initially endorsed, even celebrated, the egalitarian ethos which underpinned the Commonwealth of Australia, but was later to complain bitterly that in the treatment of the Chinese, Australia betrayed the very values on which the new nation was founded. His views, which were widely disseminated in speeches and in the pages of the *Tung Wah Times* and other newspapers, came to shape the political agenda of influential factions in the Chinese Australian elites. As John Fitzgerald has observed, it is one of the tragic paradoxes of Australian race relations that just as the Chinese were pleading for justice in the name of equality, it was denied them because, in the views of mainstream Australia, they were thought to be culturally disposed to be hierarchical, and "could not appreciate equality if it were offered to them on a platter" (2007, 116). Liang Qichao was himself an accomplished poet and novelist, and firmly believed in the power of literature to raise the consciousness of the readership and to mobilize support for the reform agenda. Along with a sharp critique of the current Chinese regime and its politics and practices, the reformers also advocated for a strong Chinese nationalism, aimed at fostering pride in their rich culture and strengthening international diasporic networks. Their agenda was firmly embraced by all of the Chinese Australian press, though there was considerable variation in their views on what constituted the national character, and particularly on the political means by which reform could be achieved. The *Tung Wah Times* maintained its support for reform within the system of the monarchy up until the republican revolution of 1911 and was frequently critical of the new Chinese government after that time. However, in the years leading up to the revolution, the republican movement gathered pace in Australia and found its strongest support in Melbourne, and in the pages of the *Chinese Times*.

Established on February 5, 1902 by Thomas Chang Luke (former editor of the *Tung Wah News*), the weekly *Chinese Times* embraced the editor's strong anti-Manchu position and support for the revolutionary cause (see Kuo 2013, 184–199). However, as this political position was not embraced by all of Melbourne's Chinese community, the editor embarked on a campaign to win support for the Chinese revolutionaries and at the same time attract a greater readership. The paper republished reports from the official periodicals of Sun Yat-sen's revolutionary faction in Hong Kong and reported on the activities of Chinese revolutionaries in Japan, Hong Kong and elsewhere. It lent support to the establishment of revolutionary societies such as the China Public Association (later the New Citizen Enlightenment Association) and their activities, including public speeches and reading clubs. In contrast to the Sydney-based newspapers, it adopted a populist, colloquial style with the express purpose of enlarging the readership and mobilizing the lower classes. Reporting on the suffering of the Chinese in Australia, it linked this directly to the oppressive regime in China and advocated for a transnational Chinese identity based on an "ideal China" with roots in folk literature, history and ethnic nationalism. Like the *Tung Wah Times*, it published literary texts and folk tales in support of its political agenda. For example, in 1904 a revolutionary play in the style of Cantonese popular opera, *Songs of Dargan Boat*, was published with an explicit anti-imperial message aimed at the lower classes (Kuo 2013, 188). And, as the revolutionary cause was gaining momentum, readers of the *Chinese Times* were treated to a novel which in 52 instalments followed the wicked ways of Huang Shang-kang while spelling out the many sins of the government and the culture of which he was the product as well as the victim.

The first instalment of *The Poison of Polygamy* was published on June 5, 1909. The picaresque story follows the adventures of Huang Shang-kang and his companions from Guangdong province to "New Gold Mountain" (the Chinese name for the Australian goldfields) and back again. It was published under the pseudonym Jiangxiaerlang. We have not been able to establish the real name of the author. The novel is told in the third person by an intrusive and didactic narrator who frequently interrupts the narrative to editorialize on the political and cultural shortcomings of China under Manchu rule. Its setting, more than five decades prior to the time of publication, is itself of political significance. The first wave of Chinese migration to Australia coincided with the Second Opium War (1856–60), which served as a reminder of national humiliation by European colonial powers, as did the addiction of Huang Shang-kang and many of his countrymen to the substance, forced upon China by colonial traders. In postcolonial Australia 50 years later, little, it would seem, had changed. The Chinese were still being humiliated, in part through their own customs and attitudes, in part through those of the European mainstream which had retained, even enhanced, the discriminatory practices of the former colonizer.

The Poison of Polygamy: plot summary

Huang Shang-kang lives in a village in the county of Xinning in Guangdong province. He takes to opium smoking which both drains his income and ruins his health. He is also cruel and crafty, not doing anything useful for his family. His wife, Ma, though ordinary-looking, is a kind and hard-working woman. Three years into their marriage they remain childless. While Shang-kang squanders his earnings in opium dens, Ma does all the household chores and takes care of his old and sick mother. Shang-kang's mother dies after taking medicine prescribed by a charlatan in the village. After their sources of income are completely exhausted, Shang-kang starts to sell his furniture in exchange for opium and his wife has to go out to gather wild plants and herbs for food. Knowing that her cousin has come back from Australia a rich man, Ma goes to his place and begs him to lend her some money. Her cousin feels sorry for her and complies. However, as soon as he gets the money, Shang-kang goes to an opium den, leaving his wife devastated. Ma exhorts Shang-kang to go to Australia to try his luck like many Chinese men in Guangdong province have done. Shang-kang has no alternative but to agree. He heads for Hong Kong to take an Australia-bound ship, leaving his heartbroken wife behind.

On board the ship to Australia, Shang-kang becomes acquainted with Huang Cheng-nan and Huang Bin-nan, two cousins from Kaiping county in Guangdong province. Cheng-nan is a virtuous and hard-working man, the closest the novel has to a hero; his cousin Bin-nan is a scholar and an outspoken critic of his country's corrupt government. After a horrendous passage which lasts 76 days, they arrive in Australia in rags, dejected and exhausted. Without knowing where they are going, 70 or so Chinese set out for the goldfields. They trek for ten days across rivers and mountains, only to find themselves trapped in the wilderness, lost and without supplies. Many of them die along the way. Cheng-nan laments the backwardness of China which has forced Chinese people to leave their homeland and seek a living elsewhere. Bin-nan is also depressed, criticizing the Manchu rulers for exploiting and oppressing the Han Chinese, blaming the turmoil in China on the corruption of the Qing government. Shang-kang, however, says that his only aim is to make money; he doesn't care who his masters are. Cheng-nan and Bin-nan realize that Shang-kang is a despicable, selfish person.

Entering a forest in search of food, the men come across a beast with a bear's head and a tiger's body. The beast is about to attack when Cheng-nan throws a knife and kills it. The next day they encounter two naked and dishevelled "black savages" (*hei man* in Chinese). One holds an arrow, the head of which has been smeared with poison, the other a boomerang. They capture and wound two Chinese, when Cheng-nan again comes to the rescue, thrusting his knife into the body of one of the attackers. The black man lets go of his victim, but one of the Chinese dies from loss of blood. More "savages" appear, shooting poisoned arrows. At the crucial moment, however, a white man turns up and shoots one of them. Frightened, the other black people disappear into the forest. It is later discovered that one of the Chinese has been abducted by the "savages".

The white man, George, tells them that they are not far from the gold mines of Bendigo. He directs them to Chen Liang, a Chinese market gardener. Chen Liang takes in the 12 men who have survived the journey, all the others having died of hunger or disease. He also finds jobs for some of them. He invites Cheng-nan to go into partnership with him in running a newly discovered mine, but advises Cheng-nan not to involve Shang-kang, who is not trustworthy. Cheng-nan argues that it would be cruel to abandon Shang-kang, with whom he has experienced immense hardship.

At home, Ma does all the housework as well as the hard physical labour of gathering firewood in the mountains. This is particularly painful because of her bound feet. It is the tradition for women in Guangdong province to have their feet bound to appeal to men's sexual fantasies. Girls in wealthy families have their feet bound at an early age, but girls from poor families, like Ma, have to help their parents with domestic chores and it is not until their teens that their feet are bound. By that time their feet are fully grown and their experience is particularly painful. Ma's mother tries to persuade her to leave Shang-kang and remarry, but Ma rejects the idea. Eventually, she receives a letter from Shang-kang which includes money. Ma is illiterate and has to ask others to read it to her. The narrator laments the lack of education for women in China. Shang-kang sends money regularly, convincing Ma that he cares for her. Her mother no longer insists on her remarrying.

In Australia, Chen Liang, Cheng-nan, Bin-nan and Shang-kang experience mixed fortunes. Their gold mine prospers, but on a rainy day it collapses, causing the death of some white miners. The court rules that the owners are guilty of failing to take necessary precautions and demands that they pay compensation to the families of the deceased. Cheng-nan and Chen Liang lose all their savings. However, they find a new mine which turns out to be profitable. With the money earned from mining, Cheng-nan opens a grocery business in Melbourne, selling food to Chinese diggers in the gold mines. As his wealth increases, he contemplates going home. Bin-nan persuades him to do one thing before leaving: establish an organization to bring together people from the Siyi region. They eventually raise enough money for the construction of a magnificent building for the Siyi Association.

Cheng-nan, Bin-nan and Shang-kang return to China after six years in Australia. This time, they are lucky to have good weather, and arrive safely. Shang-kang's homecoming is a complete surprise to his wife who is overwhelmed with excitement to see him. However, Shang-kang soon tires of Ma, who looks rather old after years of hard work, and plans to take a concubine. His wife blames her inability to bear children on his indifference towards her. She suggests that they adopt a boy to carry on the family line. They buy a baby boy and name him Jin Niu (golden ox). Shang-kang soon reverts to his old habit of smoking opium, which exhausts his earnings and dashes his hope of a second wife.

Cheng-nan, who by now owns a second shop in Melbourne, invites Shang-kang to go back and help run his business. On their return, Cheng-nan buys another gold mine and opens his third grocery, selling Chinese medicine, as well as a furniture factory. Shang-kang is put in charge of the factory, and with a stable income he revives the idea of taking a concubine. He meets an 18-year-old woman, Qiao Xi, who was smuggled into Australia to marry a Chinese businessman but who reneged on the marriage when she discovered that the businessman was 40 years older than her. Shang-kang jumps at the opportunity and marries Qiao Xi after paying a large sum of betrothal money. However, Qiao Xi turns out to be cunning, cruel and unfaithful. On board ship, she had taken a young Cantonese man as her lover. Qiao Xi's lover often sneaks into Shang-kang's house when Shang-kang heads for the opium den. The lovers' behaviour arouses a neighbour's suspicion. One day a crowd of people break into Qiao Xi's bedroom and catch the lovers together. When Shang-kang finds out he flies into a rage, but when he confronts Qiao Xi, she chastises him for believing hearsay. As Shang-kang spends most of his time in the opium den, his business is soon near bankruptcy. In order to save face, he puts a hometown fellow in charge of the shop and flees Australia in an attempt to cheat Cheng-nan into believing that the shop went bankrupt at the hands of the new manager. Shang-kang brings Qiao Xi and their two daughters back to his native village. There, Qiao Xi dominates Ma and treats her badly. When she learns that Ma, to everyone's surprise, has become pregnant, Qiao Xi tries every means to make Ma abort, but fails. Shortly after the baby, a boy, is born, Qiao Xi kills Ma with poison while she is recovering in bed. The next day she suffocates the newborn baby. The death of his wife and his son devastates Shang-kang and when he learns the truth about how they died the anguish causes his own death. When Shang-kang's clan find out about the tragedy, they are furious and capture Qiao Xi, deciding to drown her in a nearby river to avenge the death of Ma and the baby. On the way to the river, Qiao Xi drowns herself by jumping into a pond by the roadside.

Cautionary fable and political manifesto

As will be clear from this summary, *The Poison of Polygamy*, while based on a number of factual events from the history of Chinese Australia (the long overland trek to reach the goldfields, the Chinese participation in the mines in Ballarat and Bendigo, the subsequent establishment of businesses and clan associations in Melbourne), it can hardly be classified as a realist text. While the hardship suffered by the Chinese miners is well documented, the trials and casualties of this group (only 12 surviving out of 70) are exaggerated, the beasts encountered are clearly fantastical, and the "savages" hardly less so. Heroes are relentlessly heroic; villains are splendidly villainous, and get their just deserts in the end. However, the fable of Shang-kang is no mere morality tale, but serves the ulterior purpose of raising readers' consciousness, haranguing them to espouse a modernized Chinese culture and the revolutionary cause. It preaches against corruption in the Chinese government, and against many of the practices of traditional Chinese culture, especially as they relate to the treatment of women. Its explicit political agenda, while reasonably well integrated into the mid-century plot, leaves no doubt about its contemporary relevance. The novel opens with a condemnation of the practice of polygamy:

> Monogamy is widely accepted as the best form of marriage. In China, however, polygamy prevails. Polygamy makes wives depressed and thus produces a lot of unhappy marriages. Families are often ruined because the husband shifts his affection from one woman to another. (*Chinese Times*, June 5, 1909)[6]

The issue of polygamy is revisited in a later instalment in a conversation in Melbourne between Shang-kang and Zhou Suiqing, a man with a strong anti-polygamy conviction. Shang-kang, as is his habit, thinks of nothing but his own pleasure:

> Shang-kang: We were born in an authoritarian country where people are subjected to oppression and tyranny. The only freedom men enjoy is polygamy. Men, be they monarchs or commoners, can all have their needs satisfied. This is unparalleled happiness for us men. If we are as unhappy as you are, we will forfeit this privilege. A man should assert his male power. Even though his wife may be angry with him and resist, a real man will never budge.

> Suiqing: What you have said is unreasonable. Polygamy goes against humanity and violates the code of morality. We Chinese subscribe to the fallacy that women are inferior to men. Men treat women as their toys and women have suffered considerably to this day. In today's China, princes and ministers once again invoke Confucius' classics to exhort women to be mindful of their manners, respectful and obedient to their husbands and superiors. They also advocate that it is a womanly virtue not to have an education. Women's talents and wisdom are thus suppressed and their rights denied. However, behind all the rhetoric of the powerful is

their greed to seek personal gain. They constantly enlarge their harems to the extent that their wives and concubines are seized by jealousy and fight with each other. As a result, a family and, by extension, a country can be ruined. The happiness of marriage hinges upon true love. If a husband has more than one wife, his family will not be happy. This is also true of a family where a wife has more than one husband for it is impossible for a man to tolerate the existence of other men. Jealousy chips away at affection, which results in resentment. If a family is full of bitterness and hatred, where does happiness come from? (May 7, 1910)

On the subject of foot-binding, the text is equally explicit:

Foot binding is a bad practice that has been observed in Guangdong province for a very long time. […] Small feet are favoured because men like to play with them as toys. Despite the fact that foot binding is an extremely painful experience, women have to bear it. Alas, a pair of natural feet turns into a pile of stinking and festering deformed flesh and bones. Why do Chinese women have to suffer? (October 30, 1909)

Ma's inability to read the letter she receives from Shang-kang gives the narrator the opportunity to bemoan the lack of education for women in China:

Alas! In China, women are illiterate because they don't go to school. Husbands and wives cannot express their feelings by correspondence. Husbands and wives who are far removed from each other can only communicate by writing letters. What they are most resentful about is that they let other people know their innermost thoughts and most intimate feelings. (November 6, 1909)

Women's rights are directly linked to the revolutionary cause in the following passage:

Women in China are particularly submissive. They are bound by the traditional ideology of obeying their husbands and sons. No matter how hard their husbands scold or beat them, they cannot complain but have to endure the humiliation. Chinese women are the weakest in the world. […] An awareness of women's rights has yet to be developed. Alas! Women suffer in their relationship with their husbands. No wonder many a woman revolutionary strikes the bell of freedom to awaken Chinese women to gender inequality and endeavors to overthrow the hierarchy in which women are treated as men's inferiors. (December 25, 1909)

In a relatively rare passage that deals with social relations in Australia, the country is acknowledged as a pioneer in the area of women's rights:

In Australia, women's rights are highly valued, so you have complete freedom to do whatever you want to do here. (April 16, 1910)

Opium addiction is the other major problem affecting the Chinese, in their home country as well as in Australia. Shang-kang's lack of willpower to kick the habit is used to comment on the weakness of the Chinese people:

Readers, can Shang-kang quit opium smoking this time? If he can, there is no need for me to write this story. Shang-kang's opium smoking plays an important role in this novel and this is the reason why I dwell on it all the time. Let me talk about how Chinese people quit opium smoking. In the beginning, they say that they will quit but often procrastinate, and after they stop smoking for a while, they will revert to their old habit. Very few people have a strong will. (July 24, 1909)

Chinese medical practice comes in for a diatribe when Shang-kang's mother dies after taking medication prescribed by the village doctor:

Chinese doctors don't have formal education in medical science. Those who practice medicine are illiterate good-for-nothings. They have killed a lot of people, but the government turns a blind eye. Alas! (June 19, 1909)

The suffering of Chinese overseas is attributed to the backwardness of China, which is unable to feed its population. On arrival in Australia, Cheng-nan blames his country for his predicament:

> Since our country doesn't have advanced technologies and a mining industry is yet to be developed, large numbers of poor Chinese are forced to go to barren islands to make a living. I recollect that back in my homeland, I went through the same routine every day such as fetching water and working my farmland. I got up at sunrise and rested after the sun set. I lived with my old parents. What a pleasant life! Look at me now. If my parents knew my suffering and miserable situation, they would grieve. (August 28, 1909)

His politically engaged cousin Bin-nan does not hesitate to lay the blame directly at the feet of the Manchu rulers:

> Since the powerful barbarians occupied China, not a single day has passed without extortion and forcible acquisition. The royal family has accumulated a large amount of wealth. A huge sum of money has been spent on the construction of magnificent buildings in the Summer Palace. These barbarians have squandered the savings of our Han people, rendering us homeless and penniless. No wonder there are rebellions everywhere. (September 4, 1909)

Bin-nan is also the character who comments on the treatment of the Chinese at the hands of the white majority in Australia. Rather than allocating blame or lamenting this state of affairs, however, he proposes a practical solution:

> White people bully and humiliate the Chinese in Australia. We need to think about strategies to deal with this. We should forge an alliance. We should create a place where people can congregate. (November 27, 1909)

His comment is a direct reference to events in the Chinese community in Melbourne in 1907, when a conflict had arisen between groups from Siyi and Zhongshan counties. Under pressure to unite in order to oppose the White Australia policy, the parties reconciled, promising to keep peace within the community (Kuo 2013, 198).

The seemingly simple cautionary tale of Huang Shang-kang and his companions offers a fascinating and complex, if rather anachronistic, insight into the history of China, and of Chinese Australia, at two important moments in their troubled past. This story of the first wave of Chinese immigration to Australia during the Gold Rush may contain elements of pure fantasy but it is also the first to chronicle some of the achievements of these first immigrants, as well as the challenges they faced. Equally important, if not more so, is what the story tells us about the attitudes and opinions of a community under pressure to defend its very existence within the racist social environment created by the White Australia policy – views which, though occasionally attributed to characters such as Bin-nan, are clearly of the early-20th century. In terms of Chinese history, the story juxtaposes mid-century poverty and emigration caused by western imperialism and internal political struggle to the years leading up to the overthrow of the empire and the beginning of a new era. From the perspective of the 21st century, the text presents an odd mixture of attitudes, some remarkably progressive, others clearly tainted by the colonial past which both Chinese and Australians thought they had left behind. On the one hand, the democratic and feminist values espoused by this and other literary texts published in the Chinese-language press in the first decade of the 20th century are in stark contrast to the way the Chinese are portrayed in the Australian mainstream at the time. There is no evidence of their purported "cultural disposition" towards hierarchy and tyranny (Fitzgerald 2007); on the contrary, these writers are the frontline warriors *against* what they saw as "backward" practices in China, also preaching against their survival in parts of the Chinese communities in Australia. However, in their opposition to traditional Chinese culture, the progressive Chinese elites in Australia, like the author of this novel, also adopted some of the less progressive attitudes of white Australia. Racism against Indigenous Australians is evident in the representation of the hostile natives as well as in the choice of words to describe them, such as "black savages" (*hei man*), and in the portrayal of a white Australian as their saviour in the battle with the blacks. From today's perspective, it seems remarkable that in the depiction of the circumstances of the Chinese community, so little blame is aimed at white Australia and so much at China and fellow Chinese. The suffering of the Chinese in this story is due primarily to natural causes: storms at sea, the inhospitable terrain they encounter on the way to the goldfields. From what we now know of this period, hostility against Chinese miners was widespread and their ability to make a fortune very limited. Unlike Brian Castro, who wrote about the same events seven decades later, the author of this novel almost brushes aside the role of white colonists in their hardship. This may be explained by the fact that this text was aimed at the Chinese-speaking community exclusively, and it suited its political agenda to criticize members of this community and present the Australian mainstream as an ally in the fight against Chinese backwardness. On other occasions, when addressing the white English-speaking mainstream, the Chinese did not hesitate to express their disappointment with their treatment under the White Australia policy and stand up for their rights (see Kuo 2013; Fitzgerald 2007; Rolls 1996). However, in its eagerness to portray the decadence of imperial China, *The Poison of Polygamy* perpetuates many of the stereotypes circulating in the white community, not only concerning Indigenous Australians, but against the Chinese themselves. The message of modernization thus comes with a tendency to self-orientalize, to focus on, and exaggerate, precisely those practices which demonized the Chinese in the eyes of the white Australian mainstream. Together with the democratic values of the new nation, it would seem, the author of this novel had adopted many of the prejudices as well.

Notes

1. The most comprehensive source of information about Australian literature, including Asian Australian literature, is AustLit (www.austlit.edu.au). AustLit is a subscription database which includes bibliographical and biographical information about texts and authors, as well as on scholarly work on Australian literature. For information on how to gain access to information contained in the database, contact info-austlit@austlit.edu.au.
2. The authors of this article are participants in the project "New Transnationalisms: Australia's Multilingual Literary Heritage", funded by the Australian Research Council to investigate Australian writing in Spanish, Arabic, Vietnamese and Chinese languages.
3. The very first Chinese-language paper was in fact *The Chinese Advertiser*, published in Ballarat from 1856 to 1858. See Bagnall (2015) and Rolls (1996, 434). As it did not carry any literary content it is not considered here.
4. The Chinese title of this newspaper changed several times, while the English title remained the same throughout its years of publication.
5. For a more detailed analysis of the literary content of the *Tung Wah Times*, see Huang and Ommundsen (2015). We have summarized some of the historical overview and the content of the *Tung Wah Times* from this article as this is the background against which the literary content of the *Chinese News* must be read.
6. All translations are by Huang Zhong.

Disclosure statement

No potential conflict of interest was reported by the authors.

References

Bagnall, Kate. 2015. "Early Chinese Newspapers." *National Library of Australia*, February 26. https://www.nla.gov.au/blogs/trove/2015/02/19/early-chinese-newspapers.

Brennan, Bernadette. 2008. *Brian Castro's Fiction: The Seductive Play of Language*. Amherst: Cambria Press.

Castro, Brian. 1983. *Birds of Passage*. St Leonards: Allen and Unwin.

Chinese Times. 1902–1922. Chinese: 警东新报. Melbourne: State Library of Victoria (microfilm).

Fitzgerald, John. 2007. *Big White Lie: Chinese Australians in White Australia*. Sydney: University of New South Wales Press.

Gunew, Sneja. 1994. *Framing Marginality: Multicultural Literary Studies*. Melbourne: Melbourne University Press.

Gunew, Sneja, Lolo Houbein, Alexandra Karakostas-Seda, and Jan Mahyuddin, eds. 1992. *A Bibliography of Australian Multicultural Writers*. Geelong: Centre for Studies in Literary Education, Deakin University.

Huang, Zhong, and Wenche Ommundsen. 2015. "Towards a Multilingual National Literature: The *Tung Wah Times* and the Origins of Chinese Australian Writing." *Journal of the Association for the Study of Australian Literature* 15 (3): 1–11.

Kuo, Mei-fen. 2013. *Making Chinese Australia: Urban Elites, Newspapers and the Formation of Chinese-Australian Identity, 1892–1912*. Melbourne: Monash University Press.

Mitter, Rana. 2008. *Modern China*. Oxford: Oxford University Press.

Ommundsen, Wenche, and Marian Boreland, eds. 1995. *Refractions: Asian/Australian Writing*. Geelong: Centre for Research in Cultural Communication.

Pan, Lynn. 2015. *When True Love Came to China*. Hong Kong: Hong Kong University Press.

Rolls, Eric. 1996. *Citizens: Flowers and the Wide Sea*. St. Lucia: Queensland University Press.

The Tung Wah Times. 1902–1936. Chinese: 东华报. Originally *Tung Wah News*. 1898–1902. 东华新报. Sydney: State Library of New South Wales (microfilm). Index in English: http://arrow.latrobe.edu.au/store/3/4/5/5/1/public/index.htm.

(Not) being at home: Hsu Ming Teo's *Behind the Moon* (2005) and Michelle de Kretser's *Questions of Travel* (2012)

Janet Wilson

ABSTRACT

This article examines some interventions of Asian Australian writing into the debate over multiculturalism, and the shift from negative stereotyping of Asian migrants, to reification of racial divisions and propagation of a masked racism, to the creation of new alignments and the revival of pre-existing affiliations by migrant and second-generation subjects. It compares the practices of not-at-homeness by Asian migrants and their descendants and white Australians in Hsu Ming Teo's *Behind the Moon* with those of a Sri Lankan refugee and a white Australian traveller in Michelle de Kretser's *Questions of Travel*. The changing concepts of belonging in the novels show a realignment of core and periphery relations within the nation state under the pressures of multiculturalism and globalization: where home is and how it is configured are questions as important for white Australians whose sense of territory is challenged as they are for Asian migrants who seek to establish a new belonging.

Asian Australian writing and (not) being at home

The problematic positioning of people of Asian descent in Australian society has been well noted by Ien Ang (2001): due to "masked racism" there is an "ambivalent and apparently contradictory process of acceptance through difference, *inclusion by virtue of othering*" (139; emphasis in original; quoted in Madsen 2006, 118). The migrant subject inhabits a liminal "third space" being "neither here nor there" (Madsen 2006, 120), experiencing "ambivalent hospitality" that enables a diasporic lifestyle but not complete belonging. Such dislocated migrant subjectivities as seen through forms of othering – such as exoticization, misrecognitions and misappellations, as well as more blatant racial discrimination – point to tensions and contradictions within Australian multiculturalism, and the fundamental ambivalence that comes from white people no longer being positioned at the centre of the national space (Hage 1988, 19). These critiques reflect the familiar argument since the inception of official multiculturalism in the 1970s, that it is little more than a progressive tweaking of the assimilationist imperative (Dickens 2015): that is, in order to manage cultural difference, multiculturalism claims to foster ethnic diversity and equality and to redefine the centre and periphery binary, but nevertheless it creates increasingly subtle forms of discrimination and exclusion suggestive of a masked racism.

The rapidly expanding field of Asian Australian writing constitutes an intervention into the debate over cultural and racial divisions and exclusions, one that challenges the limits of hegemonic multiculturalism. The dissident potential of multicultural writing has often been noted and can be traced to the origins of the core culture, the Anglo Celts, which provides an "oppositional model" of difference (Gunew 1990, 115–116).[1] In many Asian Australian fictions, however, the Anglo Celtic core is represented as homogeneous; identities of Asian Australian and Indigenous Australian minorities are introduced to "dismantle racially discriminatory structures and institutionalized inequality" (Khoo 2008, 4) and to unmask Anglo Celtic cultural dominance. As Ghassan Hage (1988, 19, 20) points out, this often includes non-Anglos who define themselves as white Australians. Pioneering novels such as Brian Castro's *Birds of Passage* ([1983] 1989), Yasmine Gooneratne's *A Change of Skies* (1991) and Michelle de Krester's *The Lost Dog* (2007) expose subtle forms of "othering", such as being exoticized or domesticated in the white Australian neo-liberal consciousness. Yet mixed race and migrant subjectivities also show themselves as able to acquire new agency in their intersections with traditional multicultural sensibilities by harnessing or resisting the global and transnational forces which inflect their actions (Dickens 2015, 88).[2] Forms of contemporary mobilization, therefore, increasingly frame the way that Asian Australian writing renegotiates and redefines ethnic stereotypes and challenges discriminatory mechanisms by contesting, queering and repositioning Anglo Australian norms. Recent novels about the migrant experience, and especially about the second generation, contemplate a new national imaginary, animated by global forces, consisting of multiple kinds of belonging and more inclusive versions of Australianness; Miss Yipsoon, the Chinese teacher in *Behind the Moon*, stakes this claim: "We're all Australians now" (Teo 2005, 60).

This article compares two Asian Australian novels, *Behind the Moon* (2005) by Hsu Ming Teo and *Questions of Travel* (2012) by Michelle de Kretser, and their reconfiguring of new types and degrees of (not) belonging emanating from both the migrant outsider and the Anglo Celtic subject within the hybridized, creolized spaces of the Australian hostland. In referring to their constructions of gendered and racial difference and ethnic hybridity, it follows on from Wenche Ommundsen's (2012) discussion about the transnationalism of current Asian Australian writing, to suggest that the multicultural national imaginary has developed from the "ambivalent […] acceptance" that Ang (2001, 139) noted, to show alternative structures of self-determination as responses to forms of "othering" within the core–periphery binary. These signs of multicultural diversity and agency on the one hand, and changes within the white Australian consciousness on the other, can be approached from within the framework of home and belonging.

Underlying the narratives of both texts is the question of how to belong: the uprooted, unsettled migrant who confronts his or her own lack of Australianness triggers reassessment by Anglo Celtic Australians of their sense of place and entitlement as endowed by whiteness. In both, the cross-cultural encounter reverberates with the tensions that occur when ethnicity is no longer defined by home, and home is no longer synonymous with place. In their questioning of geographical constructions of home, the novels illustrate how this absence leads to compensatory imaginings: an idealization of the archaic homeland or "unlearning" practices and reconstructions of "(not) being-at-home" from alternative positions and sites.

Hsu-Ming Teo's *Behind the Moon* is a multicultural narrative of Australian city life in the suburbs historically framed by Asian migration following the Vietnam War intersected by a transnational Australia–US journey in the novel's contemporary moment. A Bildungsroman about three young people, it traces their multiple, changing understandings of home and belonging; in the conclusion, Sydney, where they meet and grow up, becomes the site of their alternative community. By contrast, De Kretser's *Questions of Travel* is a 21st-century global novel with contemporary settings in the UK, war-torn Sri Lanka and Sydney, where most of the definitive action takes place. Unexpectedly, it endorses the archaic return to the ancestral homeland of Sri Lanka, a decision which seems to undermine the cultural and personal impact of the new media and technologies in the novel. These are associated with the globalization of culture, tourism, and homeland return visits that supposedly enhance life in the diaspora by facilitating interconnectivity, increasing affiliations and enabling new forms of belonging. Tracing the intersecting trajectories of a white Australian traveller to the northern hemisphere and a Sri Lankan refugee to Australia, De Kretser raises a range of questions about the growing absence of home in their lives.

Being at home and how to be at home, issues which preoccupy the protagonists of both novels (whether seeking belonging, living with being alienated, or identifying with the ancestral homeland), are states that are constantly infiltrated by their opposite, of not being at home, or the Freudian concept of the *unheimlich*, a view of human subjectivity which Freud ([1919] 1959) in "The Uncanny" links to our unconscious or repressed desires. Associated with non-acceptance by or alienation from the host society, the *unheimlich*/estrangement in the novels reflects those problems of translation occurring at the "boundaries of cultures where meanings and values are (mis)read or signs are misappropriated" (Bhabha 2006, 155); in these cases, due to the failure of the hostland to live up to the meaning of the original homeland, and provide an equivalent sense of home. This distinction forms the basis of Jane Mummery's (2006) argument that hyphenated, hybridized individuals and communities, unlike others, are constituted in terms of practices and actions of not-at-homeness; that is "they are not at home in any attempted definitions of them by the 'they', regardless of whether the 'they' is the host, the homeland or the wider diasporic community" (38). Such alienation means that diaspora subjects also cling to more complex, idealized values of at-homeness such as continued identification with the ancestral or originary homeland and emotional attachment to the mother tongue. More suggestively, Mummery argues that the hyphenated and divided states of being characteristic of migrants and their descendants should not be configured as an alternative identity in diaspora to that of the nation state (and so run the risk of being closed off), but in the form of a more porous practice of not being at home in terms of potentiality and becoming (41–42). Such practices can be linked to Bhabha's (1994, 157) idea of the performative space in the nation culture for minority cultures, who embrace the status of becoming; and to Deleuze and Guattari's (1988) non-evolutionary idea of becoming as a reality that is involuntary, non-filiative and non-hereditary, and which concerns alliances or "transversal communications between heterogeneous populations" (239).

Both novels show practices of not-at-homeness and the unlearning of familiar cultural constructions undertaken not just by alienated migrant characters, but also by disconcerted, decentred white Australians in response to the multicultural pressures of ethnic minorities. As Mummery (2006, 42) points out, referring to a range of western philosophers, the hyphenated or divided identity that reflects not-at-homeness is in fact a feature of the human condition. But the disruptions caused by migration, in which the subject's idea of a temporal continuum differs from both the new host society's official discourses about time and those of their original home, demands some reconfiguration of identity structures. Living diasporically, as Chinese Canadian author Larissa Lai (2001) writes, is "to be without a resting place, without a home-place, constantly in motion and constantly in question" (9). For white Australians as well, perceptions of not-at-homeness often involve a challenge to supremacist ideas of whiteness based on their position of race privilege and cultural practices assumed to be the norm within the nation state: they involve semi-repressed, even violent, irrational behaviours, as well as a conscious recognition of difference. The quest for greater belonging by both Asian Australian and white Australian subjects, enacted through practices of not-belonging, leads to reconstructions of idealized states of home and belonging constituted as fixed points. In both novels they move towards new positions and alternative alignments in response to the flux of the concept of at-homeness, whether building a diaspora community (Teo), joining a globally based one, or returning to the nation state (De Kretser). These practices and positions suggest realignments in core and periphery relations, and their fictional representations demonstrate a significant difference in each writer's attitude towards multiculturalism.

Hsu-Ming Teo, *Behind the Moon*

Behind the Moon can initially be read as an assault on multiculturalism, exposing its limits as the product of a white Anglo Celtic culture which recognizes official national categories such as family, gender, language and ethnicity but which ignores more subtle differentiations of identity and subjectivity. Teo queers these foundational categories of Australian nationhood and their underpinning assumptions with the ironic self-awareness that is by now familiar in migrant voices. She focuses on a trio of young friends, the "multicultural reject group" (Teo 2005, 61) that does not fit in. As characters in transition, their search for identity and fulfilment through family, marriage, love, sexual gratification or other forms of intimacy is marred by mistaken identities, misalliances and disharmony, and further complicated by racial discrimination and abuse. Yet the three protagonists ultimately realize that reconciliation of their differences and recognition of their bonds of affection works more effectively than their individual struggles in a society whose gendered, ethnic norms they disturb and which offers only the ambivalent and limited acceptance that Ang (2001, 39) identifies. Their multicultural alliance determines a new way of being at home, one which indirectly answers the novel's enquiry into the raced, gendered and sexualized basis of constructions of Australian nationhood.

In its critique of white Australianness and multiculturalism, *Behind the Moon* is comparable to Brian Castro's novel *Birds of Passage*, which uses intertextual allusions to Banjo Patterson's ballad "The Man from Snowy River" to challenge the seminal outback myth of white male mateship in its narrative of the racialized Chinese of the 1860s gold rush. As Robin Morris (2008) demonstrates, Teo ironically reinvokes mateship as a form of male bonding and a core component of the foundational myth of the nation which developed from historical accounts of the Dardanelles campaign of World War One. This is hinted at in the poster image on the wall of her protagonist, the Chinese Australian, Justin Cheong, taken from Peter Weir's blockbuster film, *Gallipoli* (1981). But Teo's vision of a new multicultural model of union consisting of three ethnically marginalized voices demarcates an alternative politics of location to that of the original identificatory myth: "When they are together […], they are no longer living on the fraying fringes of a difficult and hostile world" (363). This asexual liaison based on emotional ties of love and affection can also be considered as a not-being-at-home practice which opens up to new possibilities of belonging and becoming; as a multicultural alternative to the predominantly male "mateship" model of being at home, it consolidates the novel's critique and displacement of masculinized, heterosexual frames of belonging which in the literary tradition have been mythologized as central to Australian nationhood.

The "multicultural reject group" (Teo 2005, 61) first meet at school in Strathfield, a lower-middle-class inner western suburb of Sydney where more fluid interconnections and social dynamics are possible than in the more cosmopolitan and elite eastern suburbs. Their confused encounters after they leave school, complicated by gender differences and their hybrid ethnic identities, undermine their early friendship as attempts at intimacy end in disaster and alienation. The novel dramatizes their independent pathways and moments of illumination that take them beyond the social stereotyping, gender and ethnic discrimination that, it is implied, have subverted the potential for finding a way to balance their aspirations with opportunity. The gay Chinese Australian Justin Cheong, described as "ordinary" and "such a stereotypical Australian-born Chinese boy that he was virtually invisible" (13), attempts to develop his body mass and improve his appearance so as to be more attractive to white men and find an "empowering white multiculturalism" (328); in this queering of normative Australianness, he eventually suffers the consequences of being both Asian and gay. Beaten up by Australian racists and anti-gays he remains in a coma at the novel's end, but realizes that ethnic, gendered labels and appellations ultimately are meaningless when he wants to identify who he "really" is.

The multiracial Tien Ho, a refugee from Vietnam, is part Vietnamese, part Chinese and part black American. Following the failure of her marriage to a young Chinese medical student-turned-artist she returns from the USA after hearing of Justin's near-fatal attack, vowing to remain at his side: earlier she had imagined herself to be in love with him. The third member is the Australian, Nigel Gibson, nicknamed Gibbo, whose obesity and lack of sporting and social skills make him an outsider at school. In order to "explain" himself, Gibbo speculates that he might have some Chinese ethnicity and that joining a multi-ethnic group might overcome his outsider status: "Two could still be class rejects: three were a *gang*!" (Teo 2005, 54; italics in original). Raised in terms of core Aussie values he goes to the opposite extreme and worries that his "not-quite–Australianness" will exclude him from the ethnic loop of "intrinsic Asianness" (61) that Justin and Tien share. He too is reunited with the others at the novel's end because his strongest attachments are to them.

Behind the Moon is comparable to other novels that can be read as multicultural Bildungsroman, such as Monica Ali's *Brick Lane*, a study of different factions in the Bangladeshi community of East End London. Like Ali, Teo develops her narrative imaging of a divided and tense inner city community by using stereotypes to indicate the positions of the trio's families on the spectrum of ethnicity and belonging (see Perfect 2014, 116). In terms of diaspora theory, Teo's narrative also illustrates what Alexandra Watkins calls "the diasporic slide", the heritage of second-generation children who struggle with their first-generation diasporic parents' lack of social ease in the hostland, and their high expectations of their offspring which make them feel caught between cultures (Watkins 2016, 577). The conventional middle-class Chinese parents of Justin, who aspire to assimilate – his doctor father, who sings karaoke in his den at home, and his anally retentive mother Annabelle – expect their son Justin to conform. By contrast, the "mongrel roots" (Teo 2005, 72) of the multi-ethnic refugee Tien prevent her from being accepted by her extended Vietnamese family with whom she initially lives, and she rebels against her mother, Linh Ho, when she finally arrives in Sydney. Teo represents intergenerational conflict more broadly, however, by emphasizing white Australian family tensions, namely the disappointment and confusion that Gibbo's father Bob, a Vietnam War veteran, experiences at his son's non-conformity. She explores the limits of the multicultural ideology of inclusion across the generations by focusing on submerged conditions of the second generation: Justin's gay sexuality, Tien's complex ethnic hybridity, her mysterious origins which lead to her search for her black American father in the USA, and Gibbo's impression that being a white Australian male is insufficient; his uneasy relations with his family evidence the reduction in symbolic value of the white Australian majority.

The novel challenges the exploitative and superficial elements of multiculturalism through incidents and situations that expose the ideology's flaws while also pointing to its potential for encouraging social improvement. Teo introduces alternative notions of Australianness that subvert "the conflation of race, face and nation" (Tan 2008, 77), and caricature national stereotypes such as fears about an "Asian invasion", associated with the White Australian policy:

> ordinary Australians teetered on the verge of victimhood, clinging on with a death-grip to a nostalgic past when unity of race had ensured equality in the nation and they cast panic-stricken glances around for someone to blame for all their gut-roiling fear. (Teo 2005, 198)

Gibbo's construction as a distorted, off-centre image of white Australian masculinity, in particular, further undercuts the "norm" that Teo's satire targets. Indeed, he represents an ironically reversed image of the dislocated, hyphenated migrant. Nevertheless, in so being he signifies he represents potentiality and becoming for, like the Asian diasporan, he prac-tises not being at home. Aptly nicknamed "Gibbo", he is "not-quite-Australian" (61) in his desire to imitate and resemble the other; that is, to embrace Asianness, so contrasting with Justin's desire to be attractive to white men.

In this characterization the novel hints at colonial structures from which the nation has struggled to emancipate itself through postcolonial revisioning, and Teo suggests parallels between the inequalities caused by contemporary migration and indigenous dispossession due to colonization. Tien's misidentification as an Aborigine at school – "Hey Abo" (Teo 2005, 29) – leads her to enquire about her father's ethnic identity. But Gibbo's ethnic iden-tification with the Chinese – "As long as Gibbo could remember, he wanted to be thinner and he wanted to be Chinese, just like Justin" (84) – by contrast, invokes the myth of the "unsettled settler", often associated with the desire for greater indigeneity and emerging as a new strand of national identity in New Zealand and Australia in the late 1980s. His rejection of white settler identity structures can be compared to those neo-liberal Australians and Pakeha New Zealanders who identify with indigenous Aborigine or Maori in order to com-pensate for their own perceived lack of authenticity and belonging; the most recent version in Australia, following the publication of the *Bringing Them Home* report (Australian Human Rights Commission 1997), is a form of "settler envy" of Aboriginal trauma (Williams 1997; Huggan 2007, viii–ix; Delrez 2010). Gibbo's acts of not being at home, then, can be read in light of the already "unsettled" structures of white settler belonging, as concepts of home, the core of personal, cultural identity and social rootedness, can no longer be taken for granted.

Teo's critique, therefore, also extends to his rejection of commonplace masculine activities, the leisure pursuits of his fellow engineering students: football, cricket, beer-swilling and military success. Furthermore, he is unable to develop a "blokey camaraderie" (Teo 2005, 97) with his father, Bob Gibson, who remains puzzled by his son's unaccountable sense of difference. But Bob in turn finds he is unable to live up to the "impossible ideals of Australian masculinity" (282) represented by his father, the true blue patriot Gordon Gibson, whose confused racist attitudes of "virulent hatred towards Asians", despite his grudging recognition of their claims to citizenship and belonging – "They've been here since the gold rushes. They're practically Australian" (279) – articulate another stereotype of white Australian intolerance and discrimination. Through Gibbo's rebellion, and Bob's reactions, the novel argues that both genealogically and culturally the idealization of the masculinized core (with its origins in the Gallipoli mateship myth) can no longer be sustained.

Teo's critique and repositioning of white Australianness climaxes in the behaviour of Bob Gibson, when his tolerance and understanding finally snap. At the "Dead Diana" dinner party, an event hosted by the Cheongs, he attacks the Asian presence in front of his hosts, his wife and son, Tien, her fiancé, and mother, Linh Ho: overwhelmed at being outnumbered, he lashes out, calling them "chinks" (Teo 2005, 133). This is followed by the realization that his violence was motivated by a wish to regain control over his territory:

> Bob couldn't help but feel bewildered by what had happened to this society, to the kids he once knew. And under his hurt and confusion there was a growing need to strike back and stake out his own territory, otherwise *how was he ever going to feel at home again* in the very place he'd lived in all his life? (283; my emphasis)

The novel stresses the intergenerational gap between parents who are rooted and children who are alienated due to the commodification of life and the binding glue of global youth culture. In overturning the stereotypes of gender and heteronormativity that the nuclear family values, the three friends demarcate differences from their parents' generation as well as differences between Asian and white Australian in order to create new space for a harmonious minority community. Tien's and Gibbo's decision to remain with Justin at the novel's end, catalysed by shock at the violent homophobia and racism of his near-fatal attack, urges articulation of alternative affiliations and loyalties. As a circle that stands for a "system of articulated equivalences" (Mummery 2006, 36), they circumvent the norms of marriage and heterosexuality which are too divisive and essentialist: "When they are together […] they are at the stable centre of the universe and life is simply the way it should be" (Teo 2005, 363).

The formation of an alternative community based on emotions and intimacy is based on what Vijay Mishra (2007) sees as "accepting the persistence of difference located in the in-between within a semantics of the hyphen" (130); that is, in a complex multicultural space where the rationale of belonging resists co-option to white Australian norms and expectations, where identity should not be closed off but indefinitely deferred. In terms of the politics of location, identity is derived from a simultaneity of diasporization and rootedness (Brah 1996, 242), a balance comparable to Bhabha's third space which can also be redolent of new belonging. The alternative community also suggests a practice of difference and differentiation that might be fitting for a new and revised social imaginary for, as Dipesh Chakrabarty (2011, 165–166) claims, newness enters the world through acts of displacement. The renegotiated concept of togetherness and belonging which elides divisions of class, ethnicity and gender risks being oppositional and closed off in order to protect its distinctiveness. Yet the novel's closing perception is that "that place where there will be no trouble" (Teo 2005, 363) is unattainable, hinting that the new community's condition of subjecthood will consist of an engagement with what Stuart Hall (1990) calls "the continuous play of history, culture and power" (394). Teo suggests by this idealization of multiculturalism the existence of Mishra's idea of "a space for a degree of free play without necessarily endorsing any ideology" (2007, 182); on the periphery of mainstream identitarian politics, the minority group will nevertheless continue to interact with and impact on the white Australian majority.

Michelle de Kretser, *Questions of Travel*

Questions of Travel demonstrates even more insidiously than *Behind the Moon* the internal fragmentation of the white Anglo Celtic core. The white Australian's dislocations due to international travel and global tourism are counterpointed to the urgent journey of the Sri Lankan subject in exile, in De Kretser's contrasting portraits of homeland filiation. In *Behind the Moon*, "home", as discovered through new attachments and affiliations in the hostland, illustrates that the diasporic subject's "homing desire" is realized in relations of intimacy between self and other – an experience that "can be attached to bodies that have touched us in a meaningful way" (Fortier 2003, 131). But in *Questions of Travel* the absence of home is experienced by the refugee Sri Lankan as the "desire for home",[3] a yearning for the authentic home, while the depiction of the restless Australian heroine, who dispenses with relations of intimacy when they occur, points to the recognition of the "inauthenticity of the created aura of all homes" (George 1996, 175).

Throughout her work, De Kretser's politics of representation registers omissions and gaps in history and hegemonic narratives through the compensatory devices of invention and mimicry: hybridized ethnicity is seen as a construction, and identities of key characters are constituted by modes of creativity and performativity interwoven with rooted concepts of place and time. In *The Lost Dog* (2007), which explores masked racism and equates race with the hegemonic national culture, Nellie Zhang, the hybridized girlfriend of the Anglo Indian protagonist, Tom, parodies ethnic difference by donning new disguises and attires and performing ethnic stereotyping. In *Questions of Travel* both white Australian and Asian protagonists move between free-floating, unformed notions of home and essentialized notions of race and belonging. The archaic concepts of homeland that Mummery sees as one feature of diaspora communities appear in the novel's twin narratives, alongside the more ephemeral identity structures that come with mobility: travel, whether through political asylum or tourism, shows the potential for a renegotiated lifestyle and deterritorialized identity.

By contrast to the decentring and destabilizing of white Anglo Celtic masculinity in *Behind the Moon* as represented by Bob Gibson when threatened by the Asian presence, and his son Gibbo, who willingly constructs an Asian affinity, *Questions of Travel* foregrounds the vulnerability of the white Australian woman, hinting at her traditional exclusion from the heterosexually defined patriarchal core. The youthful heroine, Laura, who undertakes global travel, then works for a global travel agency (De Kretser herself once produced *Lonely Planet* guidebooks), is contrasted to a radically dispossessed Sri Lankan refugee, Ravi Mendes, who chooses to return to his war-torn homeland at the novel's end. Laura, who travels from Sydney to England on her aunt's inheritance, embodies the restlessness of early-20th-century white settlers who often returned to the metropolitan homeland. Living in England suits her complexion and appearance: she is "a large white girl, firm-fleshed, the flesh rose flushed, and fine grained. The bloom that would have begun to wilt, in Sydney was ancestrally suited to England's damp cold" (De Kretser 2012, 83). Despite this illusion of belonging, she remains a sojourner and onlooker: travel does not root her into the ethnic and cultural heritage of the ancestral homeland. By contrast, in the parallel narrative, the well-educated Ravi, a Burgher Sinhalese from a comfortable, middle-class home in a town near Colombo, leaves on a temporary visa for Australia out of fear for his own life after his wife and child are senselessly and brutally murdered.

De Kretser's narrative structure of intersecting chapters juxtaposes the origin, identities and life trajectories of her protagonists so that the first half of the novel concludes with Laura's return from her overseas sojourn, almost coinciding with Ravi's arrival in exile in Australia. She is the cosmopolitan, tourist-observer who roams the world as an always belated traveller, embodying ambivalence and uncertainty. Sri Lanka is one of her tourist destinations, and when Ravi finally meets her, his sudden perception of her implicit voyeurism when he discovers she is planning to visit his country enrages him. By contrast, he is catapulted onto a path of diminished choices and undiminished longing for home; exile only distances him from his difficult circumstances without resolving his emotions, despite the gradual improvement of his lifestyle while living in the country often known as "lucky".

At one level, De Kretser is testing out the emancipatory potential of multicultural discourse in her contrasting portraits of un/belonging. *Questions of Travel* shows little of the violent racial discrimination that appears in Teo's novel, where the protagonists are verbally attacked as "chinks" and "commie bastard boaties" by a drunk on the Glenelg tram (Teo 2005, 63–65). But there is some evidence of Ang's "inclusion by virtue of otherness" (2001, 146). Ravi is greeted with hospitality and acts of kindness upon his arrival on a tourist visa, followed by an application for asylum. But reaction to his hosts is mixed: "Ravi realised that she was kind, and that his need to get away from her was acute" (De Kretser 2012, 248). He at first works at a menial job in a western-suburbs nursing home, but later, through a network of influence, and appropriately for his education and vocational training, he is appointed an IT (information technology) administrator for Ramsay, the global travel guide publishing company where Laura works. Despite the negativity of the official line on refugees in Australia in 2012 when the novel was published, and over 5000 Sri Lankan refugees who sought asylum in Australia were branded as illegal and taken to detention facilities like Christmas Island or returned (Juers 2013), he is surprisingly granted permanent residence, although the agonizingly protracted process means this possibly comes too late.

The intimacies and new ties which bind Teo's characters in the concluding multicultural scenario of *Behind the Moon*, and that suggest the greater possibilities available to second-generation migrants whose "identities are constructed with far more agency" (Watkins 2016, 578, citing Julian 2015, 113), are seemingly unavailable to Ravi. After meeting some Ethiopian migrants and entertaining hopes of intimacy with the woman, Hana, he realizes that such a relationship would have been a delusion and he turns increasingly to his family ties in Sri Lanka for anchorage. A sense of disempowerment creeps up on him, even when he develops a sense of fellow feeling – "He couldn't shake off the feeling that things were slipping from his grasp" (De Kretser 2012, 23) – experiencing the migrant's sense of inauthenticity and irrefutable alienation:

> Ravi thought it likely that when Abebe, Hana and Tarik lived in a house, he would still be only a visitor, hovering. Look at Desmond Patternot [his Burgher relative in Sydney]; he had spent two thirds of his life and still lived in another country. Ravi could see himself ending up like that, his knowledge of Australia as formal as a string of recited [railway] stations. (436)

Yet the concern with racism and ethnic divisions at the national level is repositioned by the vibrant transnational cosmopolitanism evident in the novel's global orientation. Ravi's professional training in information technology in Sri Lanka enables him to construct a virtual homeland in Sri Lanka by developing a memorializing website in honour of his wife and child, and thus to mourn their deaths. These new modes of connectivity contrast to Bob Gibson's identification with "old Australia" in *Behind the Moon*, as opposed to the "new cosmopolitan culture" to which Tien Ho seems to belong but where Bob feels he is "just a gawky tourist" (Teo 2005, 283). De Kretser's novel shows a more achieved cosmopolitanism than Teo's and globalization's transformative impact appears in the "reflexive awareness of ambivalences in a milieu of blurring differentiations, and cultural contradictions" (Beck 2006, 3); yet the preoccupation with borders, sovereignty and exclusionary identities of nation states remains ideologically influential, as Ravi's decision to return to Sri Lanka implies, and this aligns *Questions of Travel* with Teo's concluding image of unity within the national space.

At another level, De Kretser returns to the "unsettled settler" myth of inauthentic belonging, which encourages reinventions of the meaning of home (Huggan 2007, xi), and exposes gaps and inconsistencies in the hegemonic white Anglo Celtic core. Laura's rootless travel in Asia and Europe constantly reminds her of being an Australian, but on return she discovers that she does not necessarily belong: seeing herself a stranger, she views Sydney as both an insider and a foreigner. Ravi, by contrast, never comes to terms with the losses that drove him into exile, and despite signs that he could make a better life for himself in Australia, and driven by increasing homesickness and nostalgia he decides to return to Sri Lanka, regardless of the risk of being killed by his wife's nameless murderers or of finding himself a stranger there.

De Kretser's narrative shows that discrimination or various forms of "othering" occur to Ravi and other multicultural groups, but such ambivalent attitudes provoke little reaction from him (Lokugé 2016, 557–58). Instead, his sojourn becomes increasingly intolerable because of his inability to break the psychological impasse of grief at the murder of his wife and child, to articulate his emotions. In Freudian terms, his incomplete mourning has led to a state of melancholia, a pathological form of unresolved grief for lost objects which are impossible to let go. The loss of his wife and son, and then the death of his mother while he is in exile, become conflated with the loss of his country. As Freud says, there is an unconscious dimension of loss in melancholia, for the subject "knows whom he has lost but not *what* it is he has lost in them" ([1917] 1959, 155; emphasis in original). In this emphasis De Kretser creates a different image of migrant unbelonging from that which appears in Hsu-Ming Teo's *Behind the Moon* and her earlier novel *Love and Vertigo* (2000), or novels such as Arlene Chai's *On the Goddess Rock* (1998) and *The Last Time I Saw Mother* (1996) and Simone Lazaroo's *The Australian Fiancé* (2000), where alienation is attributable to racism, intolerance or mild discrimination ranging from non-acceptance to affectionate exoticization. These forms of alienation ultimately matter less to Ravi than his feelings of irrecoverable loss and fear of losing his originary identity. Although Mummery advocates the construction of hyphenated identities as a practice to be negotiated or a performance undertaken, therefore, it is clear that Ravi is unable to move beyond his historical circumstances to continue practising not-at-homeness; he returns to Sri Lanka driven by the wish to recapture an earlier version of home and belonging, entering into a totalizing horizon of identity, a form of revived ethnic essentialism, countering sensations of grief, absence, loss and distance with a belief in prior constructions of family and home.

Laura, by contrast, displays almost wilful alienation and rejection of originary belonging. Her career as a travel writer after she returns to Sydney, fostering a cosmopolitan lifestyle based on international travel and tourism, contrasts to the experience of the rooted, nationalist Bob Gibson in *Behind the Moon*, whose inner turmoil over perceived Asian threats to his presence make him question his place "at home". Gibson's patriarchal heritage, informed by a militaristic, conformist ideology, is inadequate to deal with the demands of a multicultural society as he realizes at the novel's end, yet his friendship with Justin's father – "Everyone was surprised and appalled when Bob was converted to karaoke" (Teo 2005, 361) – contributes to the reconciliatory multicultural ending. Lorna's vulnerability and tenuous hold on life is imaged in her lack of interest in putting down roots, her casual attitude to being at home, and the globalized culture and lifestyle which she has adopted. It is reflected in her friction with family members and hints of her potential victim status due to her gender and ethnicity: her twin brothers try to murder her when she is a baby; Ravi has murderous thoughts when he thinks of her as a tourist in Sri Lanka: "She loomed over him, sly and suggestive and – I'd like to kill you he thought" (De Kretser 2012, 490). These premonitions are realized in the hand-of-God ending, where fate deals a final blow and she is swept away in the 2004 tsunami that hits Sri Lanka. Here, it seems, her unconscious acts of not-at-homeness contribute to her demise.

Questions of Travel, with its parallel narratives, invites a certain reading. In place of the socially divisive, conflictual discrimination and ugly racism that appears in other Asian Australian novels, Laura and her generation represent a greater tolerance for the Asian outsider as well as displaying more limited belonging within the nation space, as global positions, values and connections infiltrate and loosen national ties. Nor do the syncretic affiliations and potential solidarities that unite the characters in *Behind the Moon* work for Ravi in his encounter with other multicultural figures. His decision to turn his back on the hospitality and limited acceptance he has found and to return to Sri Lanka, portray an experience of loss, dislocation, and idealization of the homeland; this can be attributed to the morbid state of melancholia, although elements of Ien Ang's "acceptance through difference" (2001, 139) and Deborah Madsen's "ambivalent hospitality" (2006, 120) can also be traced. Unlike Laura's mobility, which hints that the white Australian who takes national belonging for granted is in some way imperilled, Ravi's decision suggests a revaluing of diasporic deterritorialized notions of home and belonging, and a renewed appreciation of originary place, family and society.

In moving beyond the stark divisions of class, gender and ethnicity that are also challenged in the conclusion of *Behind the Moon*, *Questions of Travel* suggests a shift in the national imaginary with greater sympathy demonstrated towards Asian migrants and asylum seekers, who in turn exercise a degree of choice over what home they want. It cannot be overlooked, however, that both authors may be writing ironically in response to critical debates as Ommundsen (2012, 6) suggests. De Kretser's novel won the Miles Franklin Award in 2013, suggesting *inter alia* that its representation of plural social perspectives strikes a chord: white settler unbelonging is relativized alongside the experience of the alienated diasporic subject who, unusually, reverses the path of exile, yet takes something of Australia away with him: "Australia had entered Ravi. Now it would keep him company no matter where in the world he went" (De Kretser 2012, 264). Less marginal upon departure than on arrival, having acquired a degree of self-agency and ability to articulate his anger, the Asian figure contributes to the novel's rebranding of Australian identity as both global/ transnational *and* national. De Kretser's narratives of the overlapping trajectories of a wandering white Australian protagonist and a dislocated Sri Lankan refugee who meet briefly in Sydney – two images of estrangement and travel – therefore move the multicultural novel into a different national space from Teo's novel. Its very structure, in which equal narrative space is given to each of the two stories, hints at an attempt to symbolically realign the white Anglo presence with the multicultural marginal Asian one. In her devising of a "a more complex equation of difference" (Lee 2008, 214) between Australia and Asia in ways comparable to Teo, De Kretser nevertheless goes further in her strategic intervention into contemporary representational politics; her global novel implies that the white Australian entitlement to belong often remains unconscious (Hage 1988, 19), and Laura's fate suggests that Australians who ignore such questions about belonging do so at their peril.

Notes

1. The Anglo Celts consist of the British, of pro-Monarchist and Protestant descent, and the Irish (sometimes Catholic) dissidents. On the homogeneous, monocultural "colour blind" concept of Anglo Celtic, see Huggan (2007, 76).
2. Dickens (2015) points out that theories of race, class and multiculturalism have not yet addressed these formations.
3. The contrast between the two novels illustrates Avtar Brah's (1996) distinction between a "homing desire" and "the desire for a homeland" (16, 180).

Disclosure statement

No potential conflict of interest was reported by the author.

References

Ang, Ien. 2001. *On Not Speaking Chinese; Living between Asia and the West*. London and New York: Routledge.
Australian Human Rights Commission. 1997. "Bringing Them Home: Report of the National Enquiry into the Separation of Aboriginal and Torres Strait Islander Children from Their Families." https://www.humanrights.gov.au/publications/bringing-them-home-report-1997.

Beck, Ulrich. 2006. *The Cosmopolitan Vision*. Translated by Ciaran Cronin. Cambridge: Polity Press.

Bhabha, Homi K. 1994. *The Location of Culture*. London: Routledge.

Bhabha, Homi K. 2006. "Cultural Diversity and Cultural Differences". In The Postcolonial Studies Reader, edited by Bill Ashcroft, Gareth Griffiths, and Helen Tiffin. 155–157. 2nd ed. London: Routledge.

Brah, Avtar. 1996. *Cartographies of Diaspora*. London and New York: Routledge.

Castro, Brian. [1983] 1989. *Birds of Passage*. North Ryde: Angus and Robertson.

Chai, Arlene. 1996. *The Last Time I Saw Mother*. Sydney: Random House.

Chai, Arlene. 1998. *On the Goddess Rock*. Sydney: Random House.

Chakrabarty, Dipesh. 2011. "Belatedness as Possibility: Subaltern Histories Once Again." In *The Indian Postcolonial: A Critical Reader*, edited by Elleke Boehmer and Rosinka Chaudhuri, 163–176. London: Routledge.

De Kretser, Michelle. 2007. *The Lost Dog*. Sydney: Allen and Unwin.

Deleuze, Gilles, and Felix Guattari. 1988. *A Thousand Plateaus: Capitalism and Schizophrenia*. Translated by Brian Massumi. London: The Athlone Press.

Delrez, Marc. 2010. "Fearful Symmetries: Trauma and 'Settler Envy' in Contemporary Australian Culture." *Miscelánea: A Journal of English and American Studies* 42: 51–65.

Dickens, Lyn. 2015. "The 'Shattered Racialised Person' and (Post)Multiculturalism in Australia." In *Reworking Postcolonialism: Globalization, Labour and Rights*, edited by Pavan Kumar Malreddy, Birte Heidemann, Ole Birk Laursen and Janet Wilson, 88–101. London: Palgrave Macmillan.

Fortier, Anne-Marie. 2003. "Making Home: Queer Migrations and Notions of Attachment." In *Uprootings/Regroundings: Questions of Home and Migration*, edited by Sara Ahmed, 115–124. Oxford: Berg.

Freud, Sigmund. [1919] 1959. "The 'Uncanny'." In *Sigmund Freud: Collected Papers*, 5 vols. Translated by Joan Riviere, Vol. 4, 368–407. New York: Basic Books.

Freud, Sigmund. [1917] 1959. "Mourning and Melancholia." In *Sigmund Freud: Collected Papers*, 5 vols. Translated by Joan Riviere, Vol. 4, 152–170. New York: Basic Books.

George, Rosemary Marangoly. 1996. *The Politics of Home: Postcolonial Relations and Twentieth-Century Fiction*. Cambridge: Cambridge University Press.

Gooneratne, Yasmine. 1991. *A Change of Skies*. Sydney: Picador Australia.

Gunew, Sneja. 1990. "Denaturalizing Cultural Nationalisms: Multicultural Readings of Australia." In *Nation and Narration*, edited by Homi Bhabha, 99–120. London: Routledge.

Hage, Ghassan. 1988. *White Nation: Fantasies of White Supremacy in a Multicultural Society*. London: Pluto Press.

Hall, Stuart. 1990. "Cultural Identity and Diaspora." In *Identity: Community, Culture, Difference*, edited by Jonathan Rutherford, 222–237. London: Lawrence and Wishart, 1990.

Huggan, Graham. 2007. *Australian Literature: Postcolonialism, Racism, Transnationlism*. Oxford: Oxford University Press.

Juers, Evelyn. 2013. "Tripped Up, Tripped Out: Review of *Questions of Travel*, by Michelle de Kretser." *Sydney Review of Books*. January 29. http://sydneyreviewofbooks.com/tripped-up-tripped-out/

Julian, Roberta. 2015. "Ethnicity and Immigrations: Changing the National. Imaginary." In *Australian Sociology*, edited by David Holmes, Kate Hughes, and Roberta Julian, 90–129. Melbourne: Pearson Australia.

Khoo, Tseen. 2008. "Introduction: Locating Asian Australian Cultures." In *Locating Asian Australian Cultures*, edited by Tseen Khoo, 1–9. London: Routledge.

De Kretser, Michelle. 2012. *Questions of Travel*. Sydney: Allen and Unwin.

Lai, Larissa. 2001. "Corrupted Lineage: Narrative in the Gaps of History." *Special Issue of West Coast Line* 33–34 (3): 40–53.

Lazaroo, Simone. 2000. *The Australian Fiancé*. London: Picador.

Lee, Regina. 2008. "'Flexible Citizenship': Strategic Chinese Identities in Asian Australian Literature." In *Locating Asian Australian Cultures*, edited by Tseen Khoo, 213–227. London: Routledge.

Lokugé, Chandani. 2016. "Mediating Literary Borders: Sri Lankan Writing in Australia." *Journal of Postcolonial Writing* 52 (5): 555–567.

Madsen, Deborah. 2006. "'No Place Like Home': The Ambivalent Rhetoric of Hospitality in the Work of Simone Lazaroo, Arlene Chai and Hsu-Ming Teo." *Journal of Intercultural Studies* 27 (1–2): 117–132.

Mishra, Vijay. 2007. *The Literature of the Indian Diaspora: Theorizing the Diasporic Imaginary*. London: Routledge.

Morris, Robyn. 2008. "'Growing up an Australian': Renegotiating Mateship, Masculinity and 'Australianness' in Hsu-Ming Teo's *Behind the Moon*." In *Locating Asian Australian Cultures*, edited by Tseen Khoo, 151–166. London: Routledge.

Mummery, Ruth. 2006. "Being Not-At-Home: A Conceptual Discussion." In *Diaspora: The Australasian Experience*, edited by Cynthia vanden Driessen and Ralph Crane, 27–44. New Delhi: Prestige Books.

Ommundsen, Wenche. 2012. "Transnational Imaginaries: Reading Asian Australian Writing." *Journal of the Association for the Study of Australian Literature* 12 (2): 1–8.

Perfect, Michael. 2014. *Contemporary Fictions of Multiculturalism*. London: Palgrave Macmillan.

Tan, Carole. 2008. "'The Tyranny of Appearance': Chinese Australian Identities and the Politics of Difference." In *Locating Asian Australian Cultures*, edited by Tseen Khoo, 65–82. London: Routledge.

Teo, Hsu-Ming. 2005. *Behind the Moon*. Sydney: Allen and Unwin.

Watkins, Alexandra. 2016. "The diasporic slide: representations of second generation diasporas in Yasmine Gooneratne's *A Change of Skies* (1991) and in Chandani Lokugé's *If The Moon Smiled* (2000) and *Softly As I Leave You* (2011)." *Journal of Postcolonial Writing* 52 (5): 577–590.

Williams, Mark. 1997. "Crippled by Geography: New Zealand Nationalisms." In *Not on Any Map: Essays on Postcoloniality and Cultural Nationalism*, edited by Stuart Murray, 19–42. Exeter: Exeter University Press.

Mediating literary borders: Sri Lankan writing in Australia

Chandani Lokugé

ABSTRACT

The current Australian political and news-media agenda is very much about "outside" views, tending to treat migrants – including refugees and asylum seekers, for example – as one category of "others" devoid of race, culture or psychological specificities. A compelling aspect of literature's power is that it transforms such encompassing public issues into humanist stories whose affective and cognitive resonances transcend the limits of political propaganda. It can communicate transculturally, establishing intimate, interpersonal and intercommunal conversations across time and space. Framed by theories of multiculturalism and cosmopolitanism in the contemporary Australian context, this article looks at the recent work of two Sri Lankan-born Australian novelists – Michelle de Kretser and Channa Wickremesekera, who write about migrants, refugees and asylum seekers – with the aim of exploring their alternative understanding of multiculturalism in Australia.

The challenge […] is to take minds and hearts formed over the long millennia of living in local troops and equip them with ideas and institutions that will allow us to live together as the global tribe we have become. (Appiah 2006, xv)

Australia is "home" to over 150 ethnic minorities. However, although Australian public culture is becoming less Anglocentric and more cosmopolitan with the acceleration of migrant, refugee and asylum flows in recent years, monoculturalism continues to flourish, inciting racism leading to hostility and violence. This article is set at this controversial juncture of Australian multiculturalism.

As is commonly understood, multicultural societies are those that "harbor different cultural, racial or ethnic communities who live together in a common polity" (Ang 2014, 14). However, in Australia, the term "multiculturalism" raises contested debate because the "common polity" – the nation state – is based, as Australian anthropologist Hage (1998) observes in his critique of governmental multiculturalism in *White Nation: Fantasies of White Supremacy in a Multicultural Society*, on an "internal orientalism". Evolving from the concept of European orientalism as theorized by Edward Said, it invests in the self-appointed white "masters of the national space" with the power to decide "who stays in and who ought to be kept out", as well as to reduce the ethnic "other" into passive "objects to be governed" (Hage 1998, 16–17). Admittedly, with the final demolition of the White Australia Policy in 1973, successive Australian governments have assiduously played up the multicultural slogan, promoting various strategies that are meant to provide, as Australia's Racial Discrimination Commissioners continue to assert, "a strong structural foundation for tackling racism in Australia at a national level" (Szoke 2012, 4; Soutphommasane 2016). Among them is the 1975 Racial Discrimination Act (RDA), that aims to "prohibit discrimination against people on the basis of their race, colour, or national or ethnic origin (Szoke 2012, 4). However, white racism is strongly supported by a substantial part of the voting community, as is evidenced in the 2016 federal parliamentary elections at which the former Member of Parliament Pauline Hanson was elected to the Senate along with three members of her One Nation party on the strength of the party's extreme anti-Aboriginal anti-Muslim/Asian ideologies. In addition, public uprisings instigated by racism continue to occur on a regular basis throughout Australia, particularly in the migrant stronghold states of Victoria and New South Wales (Clarke 2016; Lopez 2005; Szoke 2012; Soutphommasane 2016).

Cosmopolitanism, as the concept is applied in this article, is a challenge that, as Ghanaian-American philosopher Kwame Anthony Appiah has propounded, relies on the practice of entwined ideals of "universal concerns and respect for legitimate difference" (2006, xv). As Appiah asserts,

> [w]e have an obligation to others, obligations that stretch beyond those to whom we are related by the ties of kith and kind […]. [W]e take seriously the values not just of human life but of particular human lives, which means taking an interest in what lends them significance. (xv)

Narrowing it down in terms of migration, cosmopolitanism would be about our maintaining ancestral and cultural roots, while simultaneously being part of the larger host community. Aware of the contentious debates around it, I use the term "cosmopolitanism" with caution (see, for example, Ang 2010; Ashcroft 2009, 13; Werbner 2006). It is conceptualized in this article as a functioning philosophy that inspires any individual, from a global traveller/tourist to a refugee/subaltern, "to enter something larger than their immediate cultures" through sincere curiosity about and empathetic understanding of cultural difference (Appiah xviii; see also Malcolmson 1998, 240; Giffard-Foret 2016). Considered in this way, cosmopolitanism challenges monocultural politics of assimilation that encourage, as Carter (2006) has discussed, "alienation and separatism among migrant groups" in Australia (338). Rather, it embraces hospitable and open-minded transcultural conversation between multicultures without the imposition of boundaries or centre–periphery politics (Ang 2010, 48).

As we are aware, literary fiction often plays a politically and culturally activist role; it has the power to interrogate the templates of received wisdoms and offer fresh new perspectives that may enlighten and transform us. Another of its compelling powers is that it transfigures encompassing public issues into humanist stories, whose emotive and cognitive resonances transcend the limits of political and media propaganda to communicate cross-culturally, establishing intimate, interpersonal and intercommunal relationships across time and space (Stearns 1995). This article examines the intermediary role that Sri Lankan Australian fiction assumes in developing intercultural conversations in Australia as a conduit into national harmony. I have selected three recent novels as case studies: Michelle de Kretser's *Questions of Travel* (2013), first published in 2012, and Channa Wickremesekera's *Asylum* (2015), first published in 2014, and *Tracks* (2015).

Michelle de Kretser and Channa Wickremesekera are Sri Lankan-born Australians. A "Burgher" descendent of Dutch settlers in Sri Lanka, de Kretser migrated to Australia in

1972 facilitated by the White Australia Policy, just after the youth insurrection instigated by the Janatha Vimukti Peramuna (JVP) that commenced in Sri Lanka in 1971. A Sinhalese, Wickremesekera migrated in 1990 when Sri Lanka was wracked by the war between the Sri Lankan government and the Liberation Tigers of Tamil Eelam (LTTE). The authors are the products of these histories, as well as of evolving contemporary Australian migrant realities. At the intersection of social activism and psychological realism, their fiction empathizes with characters damaged or alienated, marginalized or inconsequential – the ever-increasing cohort of refugees and asylum seekers, families, professionals and students. This article will now discuss the ways in which the authors challenge Australia's malfunctioning multiculturalism with humanist alternatives leading to constructive cosmopolitan cultural interchange.

Michelle de Kretser, *Questions of Travel*

Questions of Travel (De Kretser 2013) tracks two 21st-century travellers from different parts of the world. My focus is on the university academic Ravi Mendis, whose story commences in Sri Lanka and continues into Australia. A substantial section of the novel that is set in Sri Lanka prepares us for Ravi's exit from there to Australia. In it, De Kretser envisions the disillusioning effect on Ravi of the fractious racial and communal tensions that have crippled the country. When his wife, employed in a non-governmental organization (NGO) devoted to international aid, speaks out of turn, "against the terror of the terrorist and the terror of the state" (De Kretser 2013, 181), she and their little son are brutally murdered. Finally, in fear of being persecuted by the undetected assassins, Ravi escapes to Sydney on a bridging visa to seek asylum in Australia.

If the novel lacks depth of engagement with the cultural specificities of one or the other of Sri Lanka's diverse cultures (as explored by other Sri Lankan diasporic novelists, such as Ratjith Savanadasa in *Ruins* [2016] or Michael Ondaatje in *Anil's Ghost* [2000]), by immersing us unflinchingly in the minutiae of Ravi's life it provides us with the means better to understand how a country can be so crippled by internal politics that it neglects the well-being of its inhabitants. In addition, Ravi is highly individualized by De Kretser as an introvert who is also unable to claim support from any one culture or religion in a time of crisis due to his diffused Burgher-Sinhalese, Christian-Buddhist mixed race/religion parentage. Trapped in Sri Lanka's political agenda as much as by his own introverted nature, Ravi drifts existentially in a spatial vacuum, disengaged from everyone, exemplifying, in general terms, the "diasporic unhoused character" (Ashcroft 2009, 18) even within the confines of his own home and country, defined by Said (2003) as "the wandering, unresolved, cosmopolitan consciousness of someone who is both inside and outside his or her community" (53). Not unexpectedly, his great hope is embedded not in humanity but in its abstraction – the wave of new technology that he encounters through his involvement with the university website: the "digital revolution" (De Kretser 2013, 101) that, with the flight of speed, gave him the power of undoing the fixedness of place into the "everywhere and nowhere" (137) of global travel. It has the effect of effectively shutting him out from interpersonal conversation and intercommunal exchange.

De Kretser perceives several impediments to Ravi's "homing" in Australia, and through her account of this process censures what she perceives as the facade of Australian multiculturalism. Narrowing her representation down to the individual experience of Ravi, she creates empathy for the racialized migrant whose psychological growth is deadened by the formidable force of white Australian hostility. Ravi's professional personality is diminished by his first job in Sydney as a lowly kitchen hand in a care facility for elderly people. Added to this, at this place of work and in the wider community, Ravi is often stereotyped from the standpoint of white cultural superiority. Alongside an Ethiopian colleague, he is insultingly colour-coded by an inmate at the care facility: "Black shits […] don't you dare put your black hands on me! I'm warning you!" (De Kretser 2013, 291). Contrary to the stereotypical category of Sri Lankan refugees and asylum seekers – the "boat people" from the subaltern classes – Ravi is an educated middle-class Sinhalese, speaks fluent English, lives free of a detention centre, is a wage earner and wears expensive Reeboks. The employees at the care facility are confused about his "refugee" status:

> He was a nice guy but not the right kind of person; could it be that he was not the right kind of refugee? His co-workers had welcomed him with little bouquets of compassion. But the films that were screening in their minds had shown long dangerous journeys and cyclone wire. [… H]is colleagues had expected to hear of suffering. (473)

In addition, Ravi is unable to evoke the formulaic response that the stereotypical refugee encounters in Australia. Rather, he is censored by acquaintances as a "queue jumper", a status that, De Kretser ironically observes, is unacceptable in an Australia that offers a "fair go for everyone" (291). Although it is little more than a passing reference in the novel, the negative response of Australians to this "irregular" entry into Australia by racially differentiated asylum seekers, however desperate their reasons for it, exemplifies Australia's centre/periphery relationship. Ghassan Hage sees queue jumping as a threat to the status quo of white Australian supremacy. In his view, it demonstrates the dangerous obstruction by the "ethnic other" of "the order imposed by the national will for entering the national body" (1998, 113).

There are several other obstructions to a migrant's psychological settling in Australia. De Kretser is right to show that settling into a new country is a two-way street. In *Against Paranoid Nationalism: Searching for Hope in a Shrinking Society*, Hage raises the provocative question, "Can migrants be racist?" Drawing support from a number of examples, he concludes that the migrant's own mindset can adversely affect the processes of cosmopolitanism as much as the host culture's negative response to the migrant (Hage 2003, 115–119). This is evidenced in Ravi's attitude in *Questions of Travel*. While not blatantly racist, he still nurtures the ghettoized mentality that, as Salman Rushdie (1991) claims, leads to an "internal exile" (19). Admittedly, Ravi remains excruciatingly chained to the homeland by his personal memories, and this makes him unsociable in Australia, but he is also guilty of living within the narrow boundaries imposed by homeland cultural subsets that migrants carry within them – such as ranked elite, middle- or working-class social structures. Implying her higher social status in the homeland, the Ethiopian character Hana in *Questions of Travel* notes after a brief exchange with some Ethiopians tradespeople at a Sydney multicultural festival that "at home I'd never speak to people like that" (De Kretser 2013, 396). Ravi obliquely recalls Hana's cryptic self-assertion during a visit to his Burgher relatives, the Patternots in Sydney, even as their ossified Sri Lankan-Burgher idiosyncrasies ignite nostalgia in him for his own family back home. With characteristic insight, De Kretser highlights other segregations and seclusions that wall out any possibility of conversation or negotiation with the "other": "Look at Desmond Patternot [Ravi thinks]: he had spent two thirds of his life here [in Sydney] and still lived in another country" (436). Meanwhile, the courtroom scene in which Ravi's application for asylum is rejected is a classic parody of justice, and illustrates the non-meeting of cultures radically alienated from each other. If anything, this important and telling scene of the failure of productive dialogue is reminiscent of the courtroom scene in Leonard Woolf's (1913) novel, *The Village in the Jungle*, set in British-colonized Sri Lanka (then Ceylon), demonstrating that little has changed in the centre–periphery incompatibilities of the postcolonial relationship. By the time he is finally granted resident status on appeal, Ravi has decided that he will never feel at home in Sydney: Though "gift wrapped and tied with a sparkly ribbon" (De Kretser 2013, 436), he had no claim to it.

In conclusion, then, De Kretser's vision for the first-generation migrant's aspiration to feel at home in Sydney is plainly dystopian. Enslaved by the complexities of home and host cultures, racialized migrants live peripherally. They "circulate between ports" without anchor or destination, seeing Australia "through glass" (De Kretser 2013, 438). If there is a ray of utopian hope in this novel, it is for the next generation,[1] the migrant child growing up in Australia such as Hanna's little daughter, who is as yet unburdened by parental baggage:

> A boy was guiding a kayak among bobbing white yachts. Ravi realized he had just been granted a vision of paradise: it was a Sunday afternoon of a boy in a boat on Sydney harbor. [… I]t was to Tarik that Sydney would belong. The child's imagination would transform things that were of no significance into touchstones: the swamp of a summer day, the jingle that advertised a theme park, a derelict roller-skating rink seen from a bus. The city would be inseparable from her private myths. (438)

What alternative, if any, does the writer offer that may assist the migrant's search for belonging in Australia? De Kretser's scepticism with regard to Australia's well-meant but ineffectual effort to celebrate multiculturalism is visible everywhere in the novel. Here is one telling observation: "What Australia took away [from migrants], it tried to make up for with food fairs, tree guided walks, concerts in parks" (De Kretser 2013, 331). Her criticism here runs parallel to Hage's caustic observation that multicultural food fairs, carnivals and the like, that Australia encourages as part of its multicultural programme, "conjure the images of […] various stalls of neatly positioned migrant cultures" exhibited for the "real Australians […] bearers of the White nation and positioned in the central role of the touring subject, [to] walk around and enrich themselves" (Hage 1998, 118). However, De Kretser seems to make a genuine effort to construct a less trodden route into cosmopolitanism by setting the scene for several racially differentiated migrants living at the outer rim of Australian society to interweave in a constellation in which hierarchies play no part. In an interesting diversion from the main story, Ravi attends a picnic organized by Abebe and his sister Hana (former Ethiopian detainees in Australia) in celebration of gaining Australian citizenship status. Among the handful of invitees are Sri Lankan Ravi, a few Ethiopian and Chinese first- and second-generation migrants/refugees/workers, two white children, and the young woman Jodie, also presumably white. We are led to anticipate an exciting new interweave from this microcosm of four disparate cultures meeting around a woven mat. The scene recalls the reed mat as a *gacaca*, a "dialogical site" – a place of in-betweenness conducive to "discussion, dispute, confession, apology and negotiation' (Bhabha 2009, x–xii). The picnic does promise productive conversations across cultures, as when Hana offers to Jodie a bowl of *azifa* that she has "made specially", and later, when she places a bit of bread and stew in Jodie's mouth: "This was a *goorsha*, an act of friendship, she explained" (De Kretser 2013, 331–334). But, unlike Merlinda Bobis (2008) who, in *The Solemn Lantern Maker* steers her characters to attain even fleetingly what Giffard-Foret notes as the "cosmopolitanism of the wretched" through moments of "freely intersecting and parting" (2016, 599), De Kretser's initiatives are stillborn. Conversation around the mat is desultory; connections are ambivalent and transient. De Kretser effectively interprets and improvises the known and the familiar with regard to the personal losses that migrants endure in their adopted countries. We listen to the tangled stories of marginalized individuals lost between being and becoming. The Chinese migrant has surrendered his real name Rong and his hometown Ningbo for "Ron" and "Shanghai", in order to be accepted in Australia. Paul Carter (1992, 12–13) has noted in relation to migrants in Australia that one's name is an important signifier of self-identity and that its loss could be the dangerous source of one's tragic unbecoming (a theme sensitively explored by Yasmine Gooneratne in her 1991 novel, *A Change of Skies* [see Lokugé 2000]). The children's innocent singing of the Australian and British national anthems, "Advance Australia Fair" and "God Save the Queen" – that, positioned alongside one another, ironically deconstruct Australia's own uneasy self-identity caught between settler and original homelands – is rudely shut down by a stranger in the park. Overall, there is a sense of defeat. The picnic is a failed attempt at transitive dialogues between people thrown together by their peripheral status. It resembles the Internet and Circular Quay as Ravi imagines them – illusory and delusionary cities of "strangers and connections" bearing more promise than achievement as platforms of interaction and negotiation (De Kretser 2013, 284). There is no recognition or space in the hostland for heterogeneity or diversity. Ravi is an exile everywhere, utterly dislocated. No doubt the Australian community is familiar with these issues, yet the fact that this novel was a recipient of Australia's highest literary honour, the Miles Franklin, awarded for "highest literary merit" and presentation "of Australian life in any of its phases", acknowledges their impact on current Australian literary culture.

Channa Wickremesekera, *Asylum* and *Tracks*

Channa Wickremesekera is the author of five novels. A scholar specializing in South Asian military history, he has also published three monographs including *The Tamil Separatist War in Sri Lanka* (Wickremesekera 2016). Although little known as yet, and under-researched, his novels have been critically reviewed or commended by a few important literary critics in Sri Lanka and abroad, such as professors Yasmine Gooneratne, Sivamohan Sumathi, Suvendrini Perera and Frank Schulze-Engler. For instance, in an important essay titled "Transnational Negotiations: Their Spaces in Modern Times", Schulze-Engler includes a critique of Wickremesekera's novel *Distant Warriors* (2010). Discussing its portrayal of racial tensions between the Sinhalese and Tamil communities in present-day Melbourne, and of both communities within Australian society at large, Schulze-Engler commends the author's experimental engagement with one of the impediments to cosmopolitanism – the migrant tendency to build walls rather than bridges: "The social imagination present in the novel […] move[s] beyond an ossified cultural memory and towards a possible process of negotiated reconciliation" (Schulze-Engler 2009, 161).

In his two most recent novels, *Asylum* (Wickremesekera 2015) and *Tracks* (Wickremesekera 2015), Wickremesekera focuses on the second generation of Sri Lankan migrants growing up in Australia, through whose points of view the stories are narrated. This is a challenging contribution to Sri Lankan-born Australian fiction, where stories are told mainly from the points of view of first-generation migrants whose children play a secondary role. While they are not trapped in an ambivalent "liminal third space" between home and hostland like their parents (see Wilson 2016), second-generation migrants encounter their own problematics as they face the challenge of the "diasporic slide" that Alexandra Watkins defines as "the slip of the diaspora from parent-child" (2016). As Watkins notes, among their problems is the burden they share with parents of being "othered" by the host community, and the frustration they encounter with their parents' imposition on them of homeland cultural expectations and cultural mores. In addition, they struggle against parental opposition to the "bicultural", "blended" or "multicultural identities" that they develop as they manoeuvre between parental and peer influences. Such fluidity, however, also warrants effortless cultural border-crossings, making second-generation migrants potential cosmopolitans, or "transnationals" as labelled by Bill Ashcroft:

> The closest thing we have to [the] transnational citizen/subject is a member of the second-generation diaspora, who offers the most interesting possibilities [...] of the actual liberating ambivalence of diasporic subjectivity. The second generation finds itself born into a transcultural space and indicates an interesting way in which the borders may be crossed. (2009, 17)

As Watkins observes, the second-generation diaspora has so far received minimal critical attention. The following section of this article contributes to "correcting this imbalance" (2016).

Asylum

Asylum (Wickremesekera 2015) is an emotionally poignant novella with a clever satirical edge. As mentioned by Wickremesekera in an email to me (June 12, 2016), the novel was inspired by his experience as a teacher at a co-educational Islamic school in Victoria, where the majority of the students are of Afghani descent. *Asylum* offers a more optimistic view than most recent Sri Lankan-born Australian novels (including those of De Kretser, as discussed above), pointing Australia towards an exciting utopian multicultural national harmony through two minority communities in extended conversation with the dominant white culture.

Most significantly, this is done in *Asylum* through the Sri Lankan author's chameleon-like absorption of the consciousness of the quirky Afghani boy, Khalid, aged 17, growing up in a conservative Muslim family. This is an innovative narrative strategy that demonstrates the effortless transculturality of young second-generation migrants – their fluid understanding of "the other" as part of themselves. It recalls contentious debates on "cultural appropriation" instigated by postcolonial resentment of the European colonizer's harmful and offensive misrepresentation of the colonized "other". However, as Edward Said has argued, while members of one culture are apt to create stereotypes about other cultures, they also have the capacity to understand another. Going by this, Said (1993) unequivocally denied that "only women can understand feminine experience, only Jews can understand Jewish suffering, only formerly colonial subjects can understand colonial experience" (31). Concurring with Said's argument, Young and Haley (2009) generalize that "humans, for all of their cultural differences are not so different that they are incapable of understanding each other" (276). In relation to cultural appropriation by literary artists, they argue that an artist/writer who is capable of writing sensitively may produce a work of real value about the culture whose privacy the artist has "violated" by appropriating it. They note as an example William Faulkner's imaginative exploration of being African-American in *Light in August*, that compares most favourably with Tony Morrison's *Beloved* (Young and Haley 2009, 275, 277). This strategy of writing the "other" is also successfully executed by Hsu-Ming

Teo in her novel *Behind the Moon*, through her depiction, albeit in third person, of the white Australian character Gibbo, who yearns to be Chinese (see Wilson 2016). What is more inventive and daring is an author's ability to narrate the "other" in the first person, thereby closing the gap between author and narrator. Young and Haley's argument is very relevant here. They reflect that "armed with a creative imagination an outsider can even convincingly assume the persona of an insider and write about an insider's experience *in the first person*" (2009, 277; my emphasis), clinching their point by drawing support from Rushdie's observation that "there are terrible books that arise directly out of experience, and extraordinary imaginative feats dealing with themes which the author has been obliged to approach from the outside" (quoted in Young and Haley 2009, 277). As this article has already indicated, the permeability between boundaries is required for cosmopolitanism to flourish. The following analysis of *Asylum* will investigate the ways in which Wickremesekera successfully adopts this approach leading to the interweaving of cultural flows.

Asylum commences with the entry into a conservative Afghani Australian household of the Anglo teenager, Rusty, a juvenile delinquent fleeing detention. Charging into the Afghani home, he holds the family hostage at gunpoint. As the police gather outside the house to arrest him, the Afghani family decides to protect Rusty, who is, after all, "just a kid with an empty gun" (Wickremesekera 2015, 32). Thus we have members of three racially defined groups (the Sri Lankan author, the Afghani narrator through whom he speaks, and the white Australian teenager) in conversation, communicating and challenging one another on a subject crucial to cross-racial relations. The Afghani family's solid anchor is Islam. It is undisputedly their religion as much as it is their culture. The author offers an empathetic if ironic insight into the family's idiosyncratic practice of Islam through the wry voice of the narrator-protagonist, Khalid. Simultaneously, through Khalid's self-parody, the author raises questions about Muslim/Islam conservatism and ghettoization, as well as about mainstream Australia's ignorance and stereotyping of this community. Though the teenage narrator's tone is light and humorous, his observations raise awareness as to why racial tensions develop between communities. They remind us of real-life consequences of such lack of conversation between cultures that have shocked Australia from time to time, such as the Cronulla riots in Sydney in 2005 between Caucasian gang members and youths of Middle-Eastern descent. The brief extracts from the novel given below exemplify the way in which the author unobtrusively speaks to the reader through the seemingly naive voice of his teenage narrator about cultural ghettoization and centre–periphery barriers that hinder Australian multiculturalism:

> We do have Aussie friends but not the kinds that visit homes. Dad knows a few people […] and I know a few guys at the local club where I play footy but they are not close enough for us to visit each other's homes. I generally hang out with other Afghans and a couple of Lebos but friends of Mum and Dad are almost all Afghans. I guess it's mainly an Islamic thing as well as a cultural thing. But it's also a pity. You got to wait for some crazy kid to barge into your house to have an Aussie in your house. In Australia. (50–51)

> Come to think of it I [Khalid] don't think he [Rusty] had ever seen a Muslim – except on TV where they are mostly terrorists or terrorist suspects, blowing up things or planning to blow up things. (23)

> He [Rusty] seems scared and uncertain. Must be wondering what we are going to do to him. Strange creatures from another planet feeding me water before they consume me, he probably thinks. (38)

Like De Kretser in *Questions of Travel*, Wickremesekera embeds his hope for a utopian multicultural future in the younger generation. Through their exposure to the wider community that instils in them an open-minded approach to difference, Khalid and his sister Ayesha may develop a more positive and meaningful attitude towards the "other" in their midst: "We go for these interfaith thingies from school, and you meet loads of nice people. Christians, Hindus, Buddhists. Even Jews. Hot chicks too. You get them all to cover up like mum where is the fun?" (Wickremesekera 2015, 116). A complex process of ironic deconstruction of events and epiphanies in *Asylum* leads to the ultimate humanism of the Afghani family that transforms racism and parochialism into social and cultural interactions across ethnic borders: "We are Muslims and Afghans. It is against our religion and culture to give up somebody who is at our mercy. […] It is against God's wishes to turn in a fugitive" (97–98), Khalid's father informs Rusty, the "fugitive".

Generally, the author's agenda is unobtrusively didactic in the search for a cosmopolitanism that could bridge and unite Australia's white/ethnic cultural divisions. This didacticism is indiscriminately and wittily sprinkled in the novella: the white teenager and Khalid's father share the shortened name "Rusty", suggesting that they are both, irrespective of race, essentially one and the same person; all religions finally lead to one basic truth: Allah is also God. Most telling is how the author paves the way to a fleeting dialogue suggestive of positive future relationships between the racially differentiated teenagers, Khalid, his younger sister Aisha and Rusty, across the common ground for all Australians – "footy" – the most popular and iconic Australian outdoor team sport. It is also realistic, perhaps, that the conversation, at least at this incipient stage of interaction, belongs only to the younger Australians; the parents are excluded. It follows that the older generation would have misunderstood and stifled the exchange before it had a chance to breathe. The clinching point of the novel is its play on the meaning of "asylum" as it is applied in Australia. With the Afghani family offering its protection to Rusty, Australia's centre–periphery power relations are ironically reversed: the white Australian becomes the asylum seeker reliant on the patronage of the migrant family. Khalid's appreciation of his father's interpretation of his religious and cultural mores, one that accommodates the principle of protecting the fugitive, is indeed a hopeful gesture. It communicates the open transcultural space that can evolve between coexisting cultures.

Asylum thus offers a new route of hope into cosmopolitanism that is perhaps more effective than multicultural food fairs or festivals, because it offers a more intimate affective experience. It challenges Australia to recognize the development of vitally important relationships that bridge the cultural divide. As Yasmine Gooneratne rightly concludes in her review of this novel entitled "A Message for Everyone on Multiculturalism", in *The Sunday Times*, June 29, 2014, "*Asylum* […] has a message for everyone who can read and think beyond the confines of their own limited conditioning, and understand [as the characters in the novel eventually do] the value of a multicultural experience" (18).

Tracks

Channa Wickremesekera's most recent novel, *Tracks* (2015), tells a confrontational story that shines a light on a cultural subset of Sinhalese-Buddhist middle-class migrants buried in a working-class outer suburb in Victoria. As in *Asylum*, the narrative point of view is that of a teenager, Shehan, aged 17, "one hundred percent Sri Lankan, second generation"

(Wickremesekera 2015, 9), the only son of conservative middle-class Sinhalese-Buddhist first-generation migrants.

As in *Asylum*, a psychologically damaged white teenager from a dysfunctional family enters the story when he walks as a new student into Shehan's school and class. Immediately infatuated by Robbie's physical beauty and prowess, Shehan latches on to him. Shehan's quick snapshot of their differences offers a realistic portrait of the mish-mash of cultures in contemporary Australia:

> The five of us, four boys and a girl. All teenagers and except me, all mongrels.
>
> Robbie, half Scottish, half Aussie, Mark, half Italian, half Aussi, Marty, half Aussie, half Islander, and Sarah, a mix of something that has left her dark blonde, green eyed and completely batty. (Wickremesekera 2015, 99)

The young misfits spend their evenings together in a railway station, but like de Kretser's characters who meet around the picnic mat, they remain in their lost and lonely selves, but for fleeting moments of connection between Shehan and Robbie that come about mainly through Shehan's almost pathetic hero worship of Robbie. More generally, the relationships falter in the setting of the railway station which in itself is a universal metaphor for transience and non-meetings, but also, in this particular case, a theatre of violence for damaged, lonely souls hovering on the edges of life and society:

> I [Shehan] remember asking him [Robbie] once why he liked the station so much. He said it was because of the trains. It made him feel that if he ever got bored he could always catch a train and go somewhere, north or south. And sometimes in the evenings he walked home along the tracks. (38)

The novella unravels a powerful plot set against Anglo, Arab and Sri Lankan sociocultural contexts. Through the deeply private story of the development and degeneration of the highly charged sexual crush that Shehan develops for Robbie, the novel investigates the consequences of centre–periphery culture clashes. The first clash is physical and violent. It begins with Robbie's unwarranted assault of upon an innocent "Arab dude" (Wickremesekera 2015, 12) travelling in the same train as the teenagers. Regretfully, but realistically, in the outer Melbourne suburb where the novel is set, logical reappraisal of the incident through intercultural dialogue that may have led to reconciliation seems an impossibility. This is perhaps exacerbated by the fact that none of the parents of the team (apart from Shehan's) is made aware of the crisis. Robbie's actions are hardly racist in that his violence against the Arab is nothing more than an extension of a teenager's confused retaliation to domestic violence – his father's physical abuse of him. However, in the circumstances, there is only space for retribution. The Arab community pursues Robbie relentlessly until, beaten up by them, he ends up in hospital. If the Arabs remain a faceless mass that unites in a vendetta, Robbie, whom we get to know at a deeper level through Shehan, evokes our reluctant empathy as a deeply troubled boy in dire need of adult intervention. He gets a taste of this from Shehan's father, but it is fleeting and cannot sustain him.

As in *Asylum*, the parents in *Tracks* too are anchored in a ghettoized mentality; all their friends are from the Sinhalese-Buddhist cultural subset, just as all their holidays comprise return trips to Sri Lanka. They also devotedly practise the humanist ideologies of Buddhism and instil them in Shehan by subtle persuasion and loving care rather than by imposition. Shehan sums up his parents quirkily:

> They have this philosophy that is kinda weird but also cool. You are free to do what you like, they say. We can only tell you what is right and wrong, at the end of the day it is your life. Buddhism, says Dad. So they tell me that smoking is bad for me, drugs will kill me, studying is good for me, being nice to people is good for me, learning Sinhalese is good for me because it is part of my heritage, and of course curry is the best kinda food in the world. But I am free to decide. (Wickremesekera 2015, 22)

Though bored and irritated by their tactics to keep him on the straight and narrow path, Shehan eventually surrenders to Sri Lankan migratory requirements of a university education and the charm of a "respectable" middle-class girl. A small but sure move forward for Australian multiculturalism is the compromise that the Sri Lankan parents seem happy to make: Shehan's new love for a white (Anglo) girl is definitely more acceptable to them than his previous crush for a white boy! On the other hand, regularly abused by his drunken father, Robbie develops as Shehan's foil. Without the powerful parental support that Shehan receives, and deserted in the end by all his friends, Robbie degenerates tragically, passing his evenings alone in the station, and finally beats his father to death. Soon after, bashed by undetected sources, Robbie is left for dead in the railway station.

As the above discussion has revealed, *Asylum* and *Tracks* offer significant insights into Australian multiculturalism, steering us forward towards potential cosmopolitanism by advocating the combination of separateness and togetherness of disparate cultures. One feature that weakens both novels, however, is the author's attempt to pit the positives of the minority migrant culture against the negatives of the dominant white culture through the prima facie irony of the narrator. Both Rusty and Robbie gradually recognize the strengths of the Afghani and Sri Lankan cultures respectively through their close personal associations with their friends; on the other hand, the white Australian culture to which Khalid and Shehan are exposed reflects broken homes, psychologically damaged children, and drunken and abusive parents who are indifferent to the well-being of their children. By this, Wickremesekera seems even to feed the prejudices of readers against Australian culture as the review on *Tracks* entitled "Darkness on the Edge of Town" published anonymously in *Ceylon Today*, April 26, 2015, indicates:

> When we send our children to cities like Melbourne, driven by educational imperatives, we sometimes do not think of the social context in which they will be living; of the sometimes chaotic lives their peers will have experienced; of the dark side of liberated Western lifestyle freedoms and the confusions and complexities these freedoms can generate.

I conclude this article by highlighting a current weekly programme, *Q&A*, that is broadcast live on ABC TV, in which Australians are provided with the opportunity to question about current events a panel of "leaders" in their fields, among them politicians, journalists, humanitarians and artists. In an episode broadcast on August 19, 2014, the panel included Clive Palmer, a Member at the time of the Australian Federal Parliament as head of the Palmer United Party. When asked about his legal battle against a Chinese state-owned company, Palmer's response showed that Australia still occupies an uneasy and shifting ground in relation to multiculturalism. His racist abuse of Australia's close neighbours, the Chinese, as mongrels, bastards and murderers about to invade Australia en masse, resonates with the racist tirades of Pauline Hanson. A week later, on the same programme, and obviously intending to smooth the impending retaliation by the Chinese against Palmer's racism, former Australian Foreign Minister Gareth Evans, and current executive editor of the national newspaper *The Australian*, Paul Kelly, celebrated Australia as a successful multicultural society. In this confusion between the two ends of the spectrum represented by the media and political rhetoric – the successes of multicultural Australia on the one hand, and the outburst of racism on the other – is our literature that looks at gaps within our Australia–Asia rhetoric, investigating between and beyond stereotypes. As this article has shown, these three novels by Sri Lankan-born Australians illuminate the inexpressible heartbreak of the individual caught between home and hostlands, and envision roads not yet travelled, raising "the spirit of hope, and the essence of desire for a better world" (Ashcroft 2012, 2) in those who continue to call Australia home.

Note

1. The complexities that surround the second-generation migrant are considered in detail below in the investigation into Channa Wickremesekera's work, since it deals more comprehensively with them.

Disclosure statement

No potential conflict of interest was reported by the author.

References

Ang, Ien. 2010. "Between Nationalism and Transnationalism: Multiculturalism in a Globalising World." In *Institute of Culture and Society Occasional Paper Series 1 (1)*, edited by David Rowe and Reena Dobson, 1–14. Sydney: Institute for Culture and Society. University of Western Sydney.

Ang, Ien. 2014. "Beyond Unity in Diversity: Cosmopolitanizing Identities in a Globalizing World". In *Diogenes* 60 (1): 10–20.

Antor, Heinz. 2010. "The Ethnics of a Critical Cosmopolitanism for the Twenty-First Century." In *Locating Transnational Ideals*, edited by Goebel Walter and Saskia Schabio, 48–62. New York: Routledge.

Appiah, Kwame Anthony. 2006. *Cosmopolitanism: Ethics in a World of Strangers*. New York: Norton.

Ashcroft, Bill. 2009. "Beyond the Nation: Postcolonial Hope." *Journal of the European Association of Studies on Australia* 1: 12–22.

Ashcroft, Bill. 2012. "Introduction: Spaces of Utopia." *Spaces of Utopia: An Electronic Journal* 2 (1): 1–17.

Bhabha, Homi. 2009. "In the Cave of Making: Thoughts on Third Space." In *Communicating in the Third Space*, edited by Ikas Karin and Gerard Wagner, ix–xiv. New York: Routledge.

Bobis, Merlinda. 2008. *The Solemn Lantern Maker*. Sydney: Pier 9.

Carter, Paul. 1992. "Lines of Communication: Meaning in the Migrant Environment." In *Striking Chords: Multicultural Literary Interpretations*, edited by Gunew Sneja and Kateryna Longley, 9–18. Sydney: Allen and Unwin.

Carter David. 2006. *Dispossession, Dreams and Diversity: Issues in Australian Studies*. French Forest: Pearson Education.

Clarke, Maxine Benebe. 2016. *The Hate Race: A Memoir*. Sydney: Hachette.

Darkness on the Edge of Town. 2015. "*Ceylon Today*." April 26. http://www.ceylontoday.lk/96-90960-news-detail-darkness-on-the-edge-of-town.html

De Kretser, Michelle. 2013. *Questions of Travel*. Sydney: Allen and Unwin.

Giffard-Foret, Paul. 2016. "'The Root of all Evil'? Transnational Cosmopolitanism in the Fiction of Dewi Anggraeni, Simone Lazaroo and Merlind Bobis." *Journal of Postcolonial Writing* 52 (5): 591–605.

Gooneratne, Yasmine. 2014. "A Message for Everyone on Multi-culturalism." *The Sunday Times Sri Lanka*, June 29. http://www.sundaytimes.lk/140629/plus/booksarts-104929.html

Hage, Ghassan. 1998. *White Nation: Fantasies of White Supremacy in a Multicultural Society*. Annandale: Pluto.

Hage, Ghassan. 2003. *Against Paranoid Nationalism: Searching for Hope in a Shrinking Society*. Annandale: Pluto.

Lokugé, Chandani. 2000. "'We Must Laugh at One Another, or Die': Yasmine Gooneratne's *A Change of Skies* and South Asian Migrant Identities." In *Shifting Continents/Colliding Cultures: Diaspora Writing of the Indian Subcontinent*, edited by Ralph J. Crane and Radhika Mohanram, 17–34. Amsterdam: Rodopi.

Lopez, Mark. 2005. "Reflection on the State of Australian Multiculturalism and the Emerging Multicultural Debate in Australia 2005." *People and Place* 13 (3): 33–40.

Malcolmson, Scott L. 1998. "The Varieties of Cosmopolitan Experience." In *Cosmopolitics: Thinking and Feeling Beyond the Nation*, edited by Pheng Cheah and Bruce Robbins, 233–245. Minneapolis, MN: University of Minnesota Press.

Rushdie, Salman. 1991. "Imaginary Homelands." In *Imaginary Homelands: Essays and Criticism 1980–1991*, edited by Salman Rushdie, 9–21. London: Granta.

Said, Edward. 1993. *Culture and Imperialism*. New York: Knopf.

Said, Edward. 2003. *Freud and the Non-Europeans*. London: Freud Museum.

Schulze-Engler, Frank. 2009. "Transcultural Negotiations: Third Spaces in Modern Times." In *Communications in the Third Space*, edited by Ikas Karin and Gerhard Wagner. New York: Routledge.

Soutphommasane, Tim. 2016. "Is Australia a Racist Country? On the State of our Race Relations." *Address to the Crescent Institute*, Brisbane, April 7. http://www.abc.net.au/religion/articles/2016/04/08/4439686.htm

Stearns, Peter. 1995. "Emotion." In *Discursive Psychology in Practice*, edited by Rom Harré and Peter Stearns, 37–54. London: Sage.

Szoke, Helen. 2012. "Racism Exists in Australia – Are We Doing Enough to Address It?" *Address to Queensland University of Technology*, February 16. Australian Human Rights Commission. https://www.humanrights.gov.au/news/speeches/racism-exists-australia-are-we-doing-enough-address-it

Watkins, Alexandra. 2016. "The Diasporic Slide: Representations of Second Generational Diasporas in Yasmine Gooneratne's A Change of Skies (1991) and Chandani Lokugé's If the Moon Smiled (2000) and Softly, As I Leave You (2011)." *Journal of Postcolonial Writing* 52 (5): 577–590.

Werbner, Pnina. 2006. "Vernacular Cosmopolitanism." *Theory, Culture & Society* 23 (2–3): 496–498.

Wickremesekera, Channa. [2014] 2015. *Asylum*. 2nd ed. Armidale, NSW: Palavar, an imprint of Ethica.

Wickremesekera, Channa. 2015. *Tracks*. Self-published. https://www.amazon.com/TRACKS-Channa-Wickremesekera-ebook/dp/B01ER5C2VS#nav-subnav

Wickremesekera, Channa. 2016. *The Tamil Separatist War in Sri Lanka*. New Delhi: Routledge.

Wilson, Janet. 2016. "(Not)being at Home: Hsu Ming Teo's *Behind the Moon* (2005) and Michelle de Kretser's *Questions of Travel* (2012)." *Journal of Postcolonial Writing* 52 (5): 541–554.

Woolf, Leonard. 1913. *The Village in the Jungle*. London: Edward Arnold.

Young, James O., and Susan Haley. 2009. "'Nothing Comes from Nowhere': Reflections on Cultural Appropriation as the Representation of Other Cultures." In *The Ethics of Cultural Appropriation*, edited by James O. Young and Conrad G. Brunk, 268–289. Chichester, West Sussex: Wiley-Blackwell.

Tourists, travellers, refugees: An interview with Michelle De Kretser*

Alexandra Watkins

ABSTRACT

Michelle De Kretser was born in Sri Lanka (then Ceylon) and moved to Australia in 1972. From 1989 to 1992 she was a founding editor of the *Australian Women's Book Review*. She is the author of several novels, including *The Rose Grower* (1999), *The Hamilton Case* (2003 – winner of the Tasmania Pacific Prize, the Encore Award [UK] and the Commonwealth Writers Prize [Southeast Asia and Pacific]) and *The Lost Dog* (2007). Her most recent novel, *Questions of Travel*, won the 2013 Miles Franklin Award, the Australian Literature Society Gold Medal and the 2013 Prime Minister's Literary Awards for fiction. In this conversation, which took place by telephone call from Melbourne to Sydney in August 2015, De Kretser discusses *Questions of Travel* in relation to travel and tourism, the Sri Lankan diaspora, and postcolonial and neocolonial politics.

People travel for many reasons, sometimes for leisure, and sometimes from necessity. Michelle De Kretser's (2012) novel *Questions of Travel* uses the travel industry as an interface through which to explore the grey zone between a tourist and a traveller, the mystifications of both, and the situation of Sri Lankan diasporics, and refugees of various backgrounds in western locations, Australia particularly. The following interview places *Questions of Travel* in the context of De Kretser's life, as a member of the Sri Lankan diaspora, since 1972, when her family, Sri Lankan Burghers of Dutch descent, immigrated to Australia due to the Sinhala Only language policy. In this discussion, De Kretser reflects on the influence of her decade at the Lonely Planet guidebook company, as an editor of travel memoirs, and also on personal travel experiences. Through this private framework she elucidates the eponymous questions at the heart of this award-winning novel: on travellers, tourists, immigrants, the spectrum of these identities and the affects that they have on character formation. De Kretser's dialogue also explores the problematics of touristic authenticity, neocolonialism in Sri Lanka's tourist industry, poverty in Sri Lanka, the economic impact of Sri Lanka's

*This interview will be published in South Asian Diasporic Women Writers: An Anthology of 21st Century Criticism, edited by Ajay K Chaubey and Lisa Lau. Jaipur & New Delhi, Rawat Publications. Forthcoming.

Civil War, touristic narrow-sightedness, refugees in Australia, and the significance of literary accolades. This interview was conducted via a Skype audio call in August 2015; De Kretser was at home in Sydney and Watkins in Melbourne.

Alexandra Watkins (AW):   **What are the questions of travel? And have you found the answers to them?**

Michelle De Kretser (M De K):   I'll answer the second part first. No, I haven't found the answers to anything really, but I thought it was important to ask the questions so that the reader would reflect on them. As for the questions: I was thinking about who travels. And who doesn't travel. And why? What are the obstacles that are placed in the way of some people's travel? What are the reasons for which people leave home? And what are the different kinds of travel that exist in the world today?

AW: **What incited your enquiry on the *Questions of Travel*?**

M De K: Travel is something I have thought about for a very long time, although I only wrote this book recently. The end of my time in Sri Lanka was just the start of mass tourism there. I remember the first beach hotel going up in 1971. I think it had just been completed, or maybe not quite when we left in early 1972. It represented the first real stirrings of tourism. Hippies came first, of course, and the mass tourists –package tourists were about to follow. And coming from a country like Sri Lanka, which attracts many more tourists than it produces, you're always aware of that disparity between who gets to travel and who doesn't.

Also, I have travelled a lot in my life … Immigration is a form of travel. And then I lived in France for many years. First I was a teacher, and then a postgraduate in France, and later I was working in an office there, in Paris. And of course, I've gone on holiday like everyone else. I've been to lots of different places. And then, more recently, there was my move from Melbourne to Sydney. So different kinds of travel and everything that's associated with the pleasures and disruptions and the satisfactions of travel were, and have long been, something I've thought about. Also, something that is really obvious is that I worked for the Lonely Planet for ten years. I was an editor first, and then a publisher on the editorial side of things. I set up the Lonely Planet office in Paris, and later in Australia I set up a list of travel narratives. It was a literary list called *Journeys*.

AW: **Did you feel conflicted when working in this industry?**

M De K: I wouldn't say I felt conflicted, no. I wouldn't say that I was sitting at my desk, sort of tearing out my hair about these things. But I was seeing how tourism works: how it's packaged and sold as something other than what it is. For instance, the one word that was never mentioned in the office was *tourism*; it was always *travel*. We were supposed to be catering to independent travellers. Well, independent of what? Certainly not of Lonely Planet guidebooks. So my awareness of the ideology of the travel industry, a mythology really: the idea that travel is free, or transcending material origins, it rattled me on some level.

For me, travel is grounded in materiality. Most people can't travel because they don't have the money, they don't have the means. It's very simple. Yet in the industry, travel was presented as something like a dream, something to which anyone could have access, and something which enriched … Travel would change you, and you could change your life for the better through travel. Of course, it's not true. We can all see that, we just know that from experience. But there's always that hook, the promise that the next trip will change things, and that was a part of the whole Lonely Planet mythology.

Also, by the end of my career at Lonely Planet the company had become bigger and bigger. There were only 40 or 45 people in the company when I joined, and it got to well over 200 when I left. It had grown, and it had become increasingly corporatized, and that was what I didn't like. I'm not someone who enjoys meetings, for instance, and there were endless meetings, you spent your whole day in meetings, and there were more and more rules and regulations with their awful corporate language.

Still, in saying this, one thing that I enjoyed doing in the novel and that I think is important in the novel is its depiction of office life, which I think is very rare in literary fiction. Satire was the only mode I could find to deal with it.

AW: Critics, myself included, have deemed Sri Lankan tourism as having a neocolonial persona. Do you agree?

M De K: I do. In fact, I wrote about this in *The Hamilton Case* (De Kretser 2003). There's a line somewhere in there, which says something like "the colonial is replaced by the tourist now". Also, the last time I was back in Sri Lanka, in 2010, I saw it myself. I'm talking about this in the context of tourists and expats – western expats. They live the lives, absolutely, of the Raj. They have servants – they're called staff these days – but they're servants. They're waited on hand and foot. Their lives are completely separate from those of Sri Lankans except in that service sense.

An Englishwoman said to me – this was in 2010 – "there's no poverty here now". We were sitting on an island in a very nice hotel, looking across at the beach on which there were thatched huts. And I was thinking why are those people living in these thatched huts if there is no poverty? Why are these young men working like this if there is no poverty? I mean, these people, do you think that they would want to shine our shoes and bring us our meals if they had a choice? No, I don't think so. Why are those people wearing clothes that look as if they have only one set of clothes, and they wear those every day of the year? Why is that? Is it because they want to? No, I don't think so. It's because they are too poor to have any choices.

Sri Lanka, it's a desperately poor country. But not for tourists, they have a great time. If you go with western currency – your dollar or your pound or your euro – it buys you everything. So you live like a king for the time that you're there. And you stay in nice places and eat wonderful food and people are very friendly to you, because poor people have every reason to be very friendly to you. You are their livelihood.

AW: This poverty, is it connected to the Sri Lankan Civil War? And, if so, what other impacts persist because of it?

M De K: Yes. Absolutely. Sri Lanka will be affected by the civil war for decades to come. One reason being, the war depleted the economy. A lot of money was channelled into the war effort, which left other aspects of the country – education, health, infrastructure, all kinds of things – neglected; money was taken away from all of this to pay for the war. The second thing was the brain drain. People who could get out, did. Those people, by and large, aren't going back. So from the point of human resources as well, the country has been depleted … Sri Lanka will be affected by the war for a very, very long time to come.

There are also ongoing problems that are connected to civil conflict, problems which escape the current touristic gaze. I have a friend, for example, who went there in 2011. She's a very intelligent woman, a university lecturer, she spent about two weeks there, travelling around, and not long after she came back we were talking about the trip and I mentioned that I had just recently read about mosques being set on fire in Sri Lanka and communal conflicts going on. And I had asked her if she had seen any of it. And she said, "Oh no, I didn't think that sort of thing went on since the end of the war." Well, I'm afraid it does. You can go to a country, you can be an intelligent person – my friend wasn't staying in flash hotels – but you don't really know what's going on in that country. And I am the same, by the way. I don't want it to sound as though I occupy the moral high ground here. I've been to places where I have no background in that country and I have a very nice time and I come back and I wouldn't know what's going on there. If I went to Italy, for instance, that would be the case.

AW: You say that those who have departed Sri Lanka are "not going back", and yet your male protagonist, Ravi, returns. Why does Ravi return to Sri Lanka?

M De K: In terms of the novel, Ravi returns because the pull of home is just so strong for him. And also he's a deeply damaged person and he can't imagine his future differently. He's someone who is stuck in a wrinkle of time … But if you're talking about real life, very few people go back, since outside of their homelands they have better access to housing, food, healthcare, all of that kind of thing. Their children's education, their children's future, those are the classic reasons why people migrate from a country, to *give* to their children, in the hope that their children will have a better future. People basically want to live in a peaceful society, and for themselves and their children to have as many options, the widest kind of life possible.

Places like Australia have, traditionally, been repositories of hope for migrants. And yet, migration is also a downward social experience for many, the world over. People who are in the professional classes in their country of origin can't necessarily find employment of an equal level in the new country. People who are forced to leave, because of war, for instance, or persecution of one kind or another, are very typically in this category … It's the story of the man who's a doctor in Vietnam in 1979 and comes to Australia and becomes a tram driver. That kind of thing.

AW: On education, there is a personal element to your previous answer. Your family immigrated to Australia in 1972. What were your family's reasons for immigrating?

M De K: It was to do with language politics. We belong to a minority known as the Sri Lankan Burghers, descended from the Dutch. We spoke English at home always, and we'd been educated in English. And in the late 1960s the government started phasing out English education in schools. It had already been phased out in public schools, but they started phasing it out in private schools as well. So if my siblings had brought up their children in Sri Lanka they would have had to be educated in Sinhalese. This was seen as undesirable in my family because Sinhalese is spoken only in Sri Lanka. There are about 16 million speakers of Sinhalese in the world, whereas English is of course a big global language.

It's interesting, because the language policies have all reversed in Sri Lanka now and everyone wants to learn English and send their children to English schools and international schools and so on. At the time it was different, that was government policy. I had studied Sinhalese as a second language at school but would have had great difficulty going to university and studying in Sinhalese because my language skills just weren't good enough. So for all those reasons, we immigrated. My siblings left first. Then, when my father retired in 1972, we followed.

AW: Would you say that yours was a privileged diaspora?

M De K: Yes. I would say so, certainly compared to people who come now, who are victims of war or persecution. But the pressures on us were subtle and different. "Privileged diaspora" is a funny term, isn't it? Because there's always losses with migration. Everything is relative. It was the end of a world, really, for the Burghers. Over the course of about 15 years, the whole world of those people of mixed race background just basically collapsed. At independence, there were about 33,000 people who identified as Sri Lankan Burghers. Today I think there are about 3000. So everyone has gone, basically.

Privileged? We came with nothing. There was a limit placed also on how much you could take out in terms of goods. So we came with just a couple of suitcases. The other thing of course was the insurgency. If the insurgency [of 1971] had been successful we wouldn't have immigrated because we would have been killed, basically. Because the Janathā Vimukthi Peramuṇa (JVP) was anti anyone western-educated, anyone who spoke English, anyone in the professional classes.

AW: Do you see Australian attitudes to refugees (of non-western backgrounds) as having changed since your arrival in 1972? What are the current attitudes to civil war refugees, as represented in *Questions*?

M De K: Well, obviously the whole "Stop the Boats" propaganda has worked very successfully on a populist level. And the kind of person who thinks that refugees should be turned back does not distinguish particularly between Sri Lankans or Afghanis or Ethiopians or Indonesians. They are just seen as illegal immigrants, queue jumpers, etc. But there is also a much greater acceptance now, of people's rights to be multicultural, for want of a better word. And differences are much more visible these days, as there are so many more people from clearly non-Anglo backgrounds now, whatever they might be. It is very different from the Australia that I came to in 1972, which was still about 98% white and largely Anglo Celtic. White Australians have become much more exposed to people from different cultures and that's a good thing. On the other hand, I think that in certain sectors of the community there has been, because of the failure of political leaders, basically, a hardening of hearts to people who are really among the wretched of the earth.

AW: What then is your novel saying about Australia's treatment of diasporics? Is it saying that Australians are at times insensitive to the situation of refugees?

M De K: At times, yes. But this is one of those questions to which there is no one single answer. There are Australians who are incredibly generous toward refugees on a professional level, lawyers who give their time free of charge to try to help people with their applications for asylum, for instance. Also, there are hundreds of volunteers, thousands actually across the country, who work in refugee centres, donate money and goods to the centres, attend protests about the treatment of asylum seekers and are outraged and saddened by Australia's official policy on this matter. They go and visit people in detention centres, and try to help people to settle into the community. There is an incredible generosity at that grass-roots level. And I think many Australians are deeply, deeply ashamed of official attitudes towards refugees. They want to counter that attitude and to welcome refugees into Australia. And then there are those who don't. I don't listen to talkback radio that much, but occasionally I do hear it. On it there are people saying that these people should be sent back, and that they are illegal, and so on. That sort of rhetoric. There are people out there who deeply believe these things. They believe that everyone, everyone in a boat who's risked their lives to come here, is an economic migrant. It's the kind of stuff that certain politicians encourage. It's lies, basically, lies that are unfortunately put in circulation by political leaders.

On the treatment of refugees in the novel, there are people who are very generous to Ravi and who try to help him. Yet some of those people, even though they are very generous in trying to help him, can't really imagine what he has come out of, because it's difficult for people who live in a peaceful society without experiences like that in their lives to really empathize, and to see what somebody like Ravi has experienced, and what he has become as a result of that experience.

There are people, for instance, who, when they meet a refugee, expect this person to have come out of a detention centre, and if they haven't been locked up, they feel that they are somehow inauthentic as a refugee. But, of course, there are different kinds of refugees and there are many, many people who come here, on tourist visas or student visas, who apply for asylum once they get here, which is the situation of Ravi. Through Ravi, I wanted to show that there are different kinds of refugees, and to resist simplification, which is, I think, the business of novels; to show that the questions which are endlessly simplified into sound bites on the television news, for instance – that behind these sound bites lie vast and complicated questions.

AW: Could we discuss the range of diasporas in this novel, and the ways in which these various diasporas intersect with your characters' attitudes to travel? Theo, for instance, the character who's writing a DPhil on nostalgia in 20th-century modernist fiction: he lives in London, in the house of his mother, a German-Jewish immigrant. Is he agoraphobic?

M De K: I would say that at one extreme there is Theo, who is very anti-travel, he's very attached to home, and this obviously comes out of his history, the history of his mother who had to leave her homeland involuntarily and who lost her entire family. Theo never wants to leave home; he wants to stay in familiar surroundings. He is also so close to his mother and so fixated on her history that he takes it on as his own. And, when he's describing his childhood to Laura, he pretends that it is his own by taking over scenes from his mother's stories. He doesn't want to leave home because, at some level, he believes that if he does he won't return. At the other end of that spectrum is Laura, my Anglo Australian character, who loves leaving home. But one of the reasons she loves leaving home is that home is a rather sad place for her; she doesn't get on with her family, as her family is very dysfunctional, and so going away is one solution to that.

Then, of course, there's someone like Ravi, for whom home has a positive value – setting aside for the moment the terrible fate of his wife and child. Ravi wants to travel, he likes travel, but at the same time he misses Sri Lanka, because he's very connected to his family, and home has a strong pull for him. Near the end of the novel he says [in reference to Australia] "I don't want to be a tourist in my own country", so he wants to go back, and to be reintegrated into Sri Lanka, whatever that might mean. He realizes it might be dangerous, but he makes that choice. Of course he is also a deeply damaged person, and not thinking entirely logically.

Finally, there's someone like Hana, the Ethiopian woman, who is a successful immigrant – someone for whom moving countries has been a positive thing – and who is determined to make a go of it in Australia. Hana is contrasted with Ravi who, because of what has happened, can't really thrive in Australia. He cannot change his life in the dramatic way that is required by immigration.

AW: Is *Questions of Travel*, in some respects, a nostalgia novel? Is it a modern "fiction of longing", as per Theo's study?

M De K: Yes. To some extent, the two main characters, Ravi and Laura, are both yearning for something. Also, I guess because it's investigating global tourism, which is a modern phenomenon; it's connected to status, anxiety and longing.

AW: In looking at travel, your novel tackles the subject of touristic authenticity, which is a great interest of mine. What, for you, is touristic authenticity? Does it exist?

M De K: Gosh! I think being a tourist is essentially an inauthentic experience. Except in as much as it relates to actually being a tourist. I think you can be an authentic tourist but you can't deal authentically with the people you meet on the way. Because I think you're always travelling in a kind of bubble, a bubble of privilege, you're cut off from people because of the language you speak, or don't speak, you're cut off from them because of the money you have. You're staying in hotels or B&Bs to get away from it all, and what you are getting away from is real life. No one wants real life when they're on holiday. People want that lovely tourist bubble in which people wait on you hand and foot and you don't have to think about anything except how you're going to spend your day, or what you're going to have for dinner, and perhaps what souvenirs you're going to buy when you go shopping. Tourism is real; it's a real phenomenon. It's an authentic phenomenon, but it's not an authentic interaction with the country you're being a tourist in.

AW: When I think about authenticity and touristic authenticity in this novel, an image comes to mind of Ravi wandering around as an American, or, rather, a Sri Lankan expatriate American tourist.

M De K: Yes.

AW: There's a deeply comic element to that.

M De K: There are layers and layers of inauthenticity in there.

AW: This aspect of your novel – Ravi's disguise – makes me think of Yasmine Gooneratne's (1995) *The Pleasures of Conquest* – and a lot of the plotlines in there which critique touristic authenticity. When writing this novel, did you intend to interact with this previous literary commentary on touristic authenticity by other women writers of the Sri Lankan diaspora?

M De K: Gooneratne's novels, *A Change of Skies* particularly (Gooneratne 1991), were important for bringing Sri Lankan characters to the attention of Australians. And I agree with the link you're making, with *The Pleasures of Conquest*, but it really was not a novel that was in my mind at the time of writing. I'd read quite a lot of studies of tourism and travel when I was working on the book, and I wanted to write seriously about tourism, but I also wanted it to be funny, as a way of getting my point across. The authors of scholarly studies often seem, and understandably so, to be taking a rather moral high ground in their attitude towards tourism and I didn't like that. As for other novels about tourism: I remember years ago reading David Lodge's (1991) *Paradise News*. It's about being a tourist in Hawaii. It's a very funny and very satirical book, which resonated with me. So, it's a funny sort of thing because on the one hand I wanted to write about the hypocrisy of tourism and the mythology that sustains the tourism industry, but I also wanted to write about the pleasures people derive from being a tourist.

AW: This is such a tragicomic novel. It's steeped in parody yet dealing with complex and difficult situations. Comedy and tragedy – are they wholly congruent?

M De K: I think so. I suppose I am drawn to writers who mix those two and so they come out in my own work. You know, a phenomenon like tourism is tragicomic, by definition. So the subject matter really lent itself to that. So yes. I would say they are definitely congruent.

AW: In *Questions*, you frame the Internet as a modern travel space. Will you speak about this? How does the Internet diminish barriers of distance? Is it an effective or ineffective substitute for actual presence? And, on this, I have a particular episode from the book in mind: Ravi's mother's online funeral.

M De K: I think on the one hand, obviously, people can stay in touch more easily than before. When I came to Australia, you felt the distance. You felt the many thousands of miles between Melbourne and Colombo, and the Internet certainly diminishes that.

Also, for instance, if you're living in a country where you have no hope of travel because you don't have the money, the Internet offers you access to images of other places, other countries and other lives. It shows you other worlds in a way that nothing else did before. The movies were the first to do it, I suppose, but the Internet does it more completely, and more often. On the other hand, this technology, it can make you dissatisfied with your own life, as you feel the difference between your own life and life in other places more acutely when you can have unlimited access to those images. So I don't think it is really an entirely satisfying substitute for presence.

AW: What significance do literary accolades have for you, such as the Miles Franklin, which you won for *Questions*?

M De K: The Miles Franklin Award means that I don't wake up at three in the morning worried about money. That's on a very basic and practical level. But look, on the one hand, I just think all prizes are a hideous lottery, really, and it could have easily gone to one of the other books on the list, which were all worthy. On the other hand, this award makes me feel that there is a place for me in Australian literature. Because it is the Miles and it has that iconic feeling about it. And because for so long – for so, so long – my book wouldn't have even been eligible for it, because previously they only wanted books set entirely in Australia. Which is just crazy really. But that's the way the trust was set up. So through this award, I felt as if my writing had been recognized as being Australian writing.

AW: And thus, that Australia is finally recognizing the significance of its multicultural literary outputs or identities, through your book? Does this perhaps signify progress on a national level regarding multiculturalism?

M De K: That's a large significance for any novel to bear! You might well be right, but I prefer to think that I won the Miles because the judges thought that it was a good novel. I think that over a long time, critics, scholars, readers of all kinds quietly lobbied to have the eligibility criteria of the Miles broadened, to include works "portraying Australian life in any of its phases". That change finally happened before my novel was published, so I don't think my work had anything to do with it. Still, this change, it benefited me and it was an important move towards inclusivity in Australia's literary culture.

Disclosure statement

No potential conflict of interest was reported by the author.

References

De Kretser, Michelle. 2003. *The Hamilton Case*. Sydney: Knopf.
De Kretser, Michelle. 2012. *Questions of Travel*. Sydney: Allen and Unwin.
Gooneratne, Yasmine. 1991. *A Change of Skies*. Sydney: Pan Macmillan.
Gooneratne, Yasmine. 1995. *The Pleasures of Conquest*. New Delhi: Penguin.
Lodge, David. 1991. *Paradise News*. London: Secker and Warburg.

The diasporic slide: representations of second-generation diasporas in Yasmine Gooneratne's *A Change of Skies* (1991) and in Chandani Lokugé's *If the Moon Smiled* (2000) and *Softly as I Leave You* (2011)

Alexandra Watkins

ABSTRACT

The novels by Yasmine Gooneratne, *A Change of Skies* (1991), and Chandani Lokugé, *If the Moon Smiled* (2000) and *Softly as I Leave You* (2011), show the challenge of diaspora as sliding from parents to children. These fictions portray second-generation immigrants as "caught between two cultures": the Sri Lankan culture of their parents and the Australian culture with which they engage at school and university. In Gooneratne's comedy this cultural negotiation creates comic ambivalence in the second-generation character Veena, who is set to repeat the actions of her forebears. Gooneratne's playful outcome contrasts with Lokugé's tragic vision in her novels *If the Moon Smiled* and *Softly as I Leave You*, which position the "model minority" stereotype and racism in Australia, respectively, as significant challenges for second-generation characters. This article aims to counterbalance the dominant critical focus on first-generation diaspora in fiction. It examines relationships between parent and child characters in the novels in the context of social studies on second-generation diaspora, the South Asian diaspora, and multiculturalism in Australia.

Paradigmatically, diaspora is slippery. As a term, it is chiefly used to describe the experience of immigrants who have been forced to leave their homeland (Watkins 2015, 165). It is also used more generally to describe the condition of being an immigrant: the act of negotiating old and new identities, in a practical sense as well as psychologically. The diasporic condition is also inevitably inherited, affecting the children of immigrants, a problematic which has to date received less attention than first-generation diaspora analyses. This article works to correct this imbalance by surveying the challenges of what I call "the diasporic slide": the slip of diaspora from parent to child. Specifically, it will analyse representations of second-generation diasporas in Yasmine Gooneratne's (1991) *A Change of Skies* and in Chandani Lokugé's novels *If the Moon Smiled* (Lokugé 2000) and *Softly as I Leave You* (Lokugé 2011a). This study will contrast Gooneratne's comic representation of the second-generation diaspora in the "epilogue" of *A Change of Skies* with the second-generation tragedies of Lokugé's novels. It will examine the weight of diasporic affect by focusing on relationships between parent and child characters, and the issues that shape their various world views. These views will also be considered in relation to social theory on second-generation diaspora, the South Asian diaspora, and multiculturalism in Australia.

Critics vary in opinion over the validity of the concept of second-generation diasporas. Sociologists Sharon K. Houseknecht and Jerry G. Pankhurst (2000) believe that in contrast to their parents, the children of South Asian immigrants are definitely not diasporic, "not caught between two cultures" (284), suggesting instead that they "are active scribes – communicating the new culture to the old and the old to the new" (285). Ellie Vasta (1993), discussing immigrants in Australia, concurs, describing many second-generation migrants as "cultural brokers for their ethnic communities and groups" who have "double cultural competencies" (220) regardless of cultural ambivalence experiences. Roberta Julian (2015), writing in *Australian Sociology*, develops a similar theory. Following Vasta, Julian suggests that in Australia "the increased acceptance of cultural diversity associated with multiculturalism [policies] has allowed identities to be constructed with far more agency on the part of the second generation". She argues that "second generational men and women are far more comfortable with bicultural identities […] blended identities […] and multicultural identities" than first-generation immigrants (113).

In contrast, Mette Louise Berg and Susan Eckstein (1991), in "Reimagining Migrant Generations", observe the seriousness of second-generation diasporas. They recommend a "diaspora framework" for approaching intergenerational diasporas (8). As they explain:

> The diaspora frame […] captures symbolic engagement across country borders that may be very real in its consequences. As such, the diaspora framework helps account for homeland identities and commitments that remain meaningful even when migrants or their descendants' direct ties to their homeland subside, when migrants have very little or no direct experience of the homeland to which they lay claim, or when the homeland is purely imagined. (7)

Berg and Eckstein believe that parents "can pass down to their children (and their children's children, etc.) their generation's […] interpretations of the past [, … their] thoughts, perspectives, and practices" (10). Fiction dealing with second-generation diasporas reflects this, in part, but not absolutely. While suggesting that diaspora is a real issue for second-generation diasporics, such fiction predominantly presents the frustration and challenge when negotiating the cultural expectations of parents in contrast to "host" cultures. It suggests that while second-generation diasporics are decidedly more comfortable with "bicultural identities", as Roberta Julian (2015, 113) suggests, they struggle significantly with their parents' inability to achieve this degree of comfort, and also with parental expectations which keep them torn between two cultures. Issues such as "model minority" stereotypes and racism are represented as significant challenges for young adults in fiction that explores second-generation diasporas. These issues will now be discussed in the context of the South Asian diaspora in Australia, America, and Britain.

Model minorities vs. racial "Others"

According to Alice Pung (2008) in *Growing up Asian in Australia*, the "Model Minority" stereotype is problematic for Asian Australian children. As Pung explains, Asian Australians are sometimes perceived as

[the] "model minority", working hard, studying hard, conforming to the expectations and ideals of the dominant culture [... which] can be a burden for young Asian-Australians growing up. It implies that external indicators of success – money, education, fame, career – define the value of [... their] contribution to society. (4)

Pung is one of many writers who criticize the "burden" of the "model minority" stereotype, a concept that was coined in the mid-1960s in America to describe the successes of America's Japanese and Chinese minority groups (Wu 2014, 2). This stereotype has since become blanket terminology for nearly all Asian diaspora communities in America, and other western locations, including Australia and Britain. A number of publications, mainly by Americans, examine the problematics of racism in the stereotype, due to the way it homogenizes and cubbyholes diverse communities. Examples include Rupam Saran's *Navigating Model Minority Stereotypes: Asian Indian Youth in South Asian Diaspora* (2016), Nicholas Hartlep's *Modern Societal Impacts of the Model Minority Stereotype* (2015), Ellen Wu's *The Color of Success: Asian Americans and the Origins of the Model Minority* (2014), and Stacey Lee's *Unravelling the Model Minority Stereotype* (2009). Saran's *Navigating Model Minority Stereotypes*, in particular, suggests that the model minority stereotype is now the greatest psychological burden in the US for young Americans with South Asian cultural affiliations; anti-Asian racism is second to this (Saran 2016, 153). Saran argues that this "burden" is particularly hard for low academic achievers. For this demographic "the pressure of such high expectations [... causes] depression, anxiety, and rebellion" (179). Fiction by Australia women writers of the Sri Lankan diaspora indicates that these American "model minority" issues also appear in Australia.

Race and colour as diaspora slide indicators

Analysis of generation diasporas often focuses on race and colour as diaspora slide indicators. Carole Tan (2006), for example, in "The Tyranny of Appearance: Chinese Australian Identities and the Politics of Difference" discusses the problematics of race and colour as markers of difference for Asian Australians: "the tyrannising power of race and looks [shapes] the experience of multi-generational [Asian] Australians [by] obstructing their acceptance as 'real' Australians within mainstream society" (77). She sees

this tyrannising power [as stemming] from the conflation of "race, face, and nation" within Australian discourse in which "whiteness" and "Australianness" are seen as synonymous and "Asian looks" become invested with notions of "foreignness" and "un-Australianness". [...] The ramifications of this are significant [...] when it leads to [outbreaks of] hostility and racism. (77)

Tan refers specifically to attacks upon Chinese Australians, although the hostility stretches further. Indeed, one does not have to look far into collective memory to find examples of other Asian groups who have been targeted and vilified, especially since 9/11. Since then, there has been a resurgence in racism against various Asian diaspora communities in Australia and internationally, who have been positioned by national and international governments and media sources as security threats. In "The Remaking of a Model Minority", Jaspit Puar and Amir Rai (2004) discuss this phenomenon in the British context, suggesting that South Asians have been repositioned by fear campaigns concerning the Muslim/Arab terrorist and that "the model minority status of South Asians has now been tarnished [by] association with Osama Bin Laden and other terrorist figures" (81). Anita Harris (2013) in

Young People and Everyday Multiculturalism indicates that second-generation immigrants are the worst affected by the international backlash against Muslim communities since 9/11 and that the reactive focus on integration and assimilation for them and "Muslim immigrants in particular [has] constructed [young people] as potential threats to the state […] whose citizenship and expressions of national loyalty must be carefully managed and monitored" (117).

The slip of diaspora in fiction

By contrast to the proliferation of first-generation diasporas in South Asian diaspora fiction, representations of second-generation diasporas are relatively few. Jhumpa Lahiri and Monica Ali are both known for their contribution to fiction of the Indian diaspora, and women's fiction of the Bangladeshi diaspora respectively, and for their explorations of tensions between first- and second-generation diasporics (Field 2004, 169; A.F.M. Maswood 2012, 103). V.V. Ganeshananthan, a writer of American women's fiction of the Sri Lankan diaspora, is another significant name; her *Love Marriage* (2009) examines the trope of diasporic "double consciousness" through a second-generation protagonist who is deeply disturbed by the arrival of Tamil "terrorist" relatives (Watkins 2015, 200). The significance of Yasmine Gooneratne and Chandani Lokugé (both Sinhalese Australian Sri Lankan diaspora writers) in representing second-generation diasporas has so far been overlooked (Watkins 2015, 5–7); the following discussion aims to correct this omission with reference to Gooneratne's (1991) *A Change of Skies* and Lokugé's *If the Moon Smiled* (Lokugé 2000a) and *Softly as I Leave You* (Lokugé 2011a), novels which provide a uniquely Australian perspective on the second-generation diasporic condition.

A Change of Skies

Yasmine Gooneratne's (1991) *A Change of Skies* is an outrageously zany Asian Australian immigration comedy, which is notable as the first novel of its kind to bring, in Michelle de Kretser's words, "Sri Lankan characters to the attention of Australians" (De Kretser 2016). This novel emerged out of Australia's positive multiculturalism political climate in the late 1980s, when multiculturalism was suddenly fashionable in literature, theatre, and television, albeit tempered with comedy (Davis 2009, 20–22).[1] It introduced Australians to the whacky Asian duo, Bharat and Navaranjini Mangala-Davasinha, a married Sri Lankan pair who move to Sydney during the 1960s. The "White Australia Policy" is still in force upon their arrival, but they are unaffected by it.[2] They are welcomed to the country as "honorary whites" because of Bharat's academic profile as a visiting lecturer in linguistics (Gooneratne 1991, 33). They struggle initially with their cultural differences in Australia, which lead them to adopt "fishy" "Aussie" names – Barry and Jean Mundy – a comic scenario that has been well critiqued (Lokugé 2000b; Watkins 2015). Their mad antics provide a "screwball" battle-of-the-sexes Asian-Aussie tale, lampooning intellectualism, whilst skilfully interrogating issues of racism in Australia and their effects on new immigrants, highlighted through a parallel storyline about Edward, Bharat's grandfather. The novel's final chapter, its "epilogue", is a significant continuation of Gooneratne's multicultural comment, although previously overlooked by critics. It involves the second-generation story of Edwina/Veena, the daughter of the protagonists "Barry and Jean" who, as she explains, died in a plane crash a few years earlier (in a doubled "death of the author" dénouement). Edwina/Veena, a university student, is now boldly boarding a plane to Sri Lanka. This addendum explores her various contradictions, as a second-generation diasporic.

Edwina/Veena describes herself as a "hyphenated Australian" (Gooneratne 1991, 312) living, despite the findings of Houseknecht and Pankhurst (2000), "betwixt and between" bicultural identities (285). Her mainstream Australian identity is worn at home for Aunty Maureen and Uncle Bruce, the Australian family friends she lives with following the death of her parents, and her "exotic" Asian identity is worn outside home, indicated by her on-campus name "Veena […] like the musical instrument" (317), an alias that she swiftly adopts on her first day at university. She explains this transformation as adapting to the expectations of her cosmopolitan classmates who, as Gooneratne satirizes, are well acquainted with Indian music in vogue and keen connoisseurs of Asian takeaway foods (317). Veena/Edwina elucidates:

> The kids at uni go into shock horror mode in a major way when they find out about my Christmases with Aunty Maureen and Uncle Bruce. "But whatever do *you* do *there*, Veena?" they ask. They can't square the Christmases that they know with "exotic" me. […] I feel a bit guilty about these conversations, disloyal to Aunty Maureen and Uncle Bruce. Because the truth is, I'd never miss one of their Christmas parties. Never. No way. But you've got to do a bit of acting when you live between two cultures. You've got to protect your image. (316; emphasis in the original)

Veena's observation about acting is reminiscent of certain theories of identity and cultural identity as performance (see Brewster 1995, 88; Bhabha 1994, 2; Butler 1993, 140; Richardson 2015, 15), ideas that are likewise suggested by the identity performances of other characters, Barry Mundy (Veena's father) especially. Representation of cultural identities as performance also appears in Gooneratne's subsequent novel, *The Pleasures of Conquest* (1996), which examines the circus of touristic exoticism in Sri Lanka (see Watkins 2015, 151–164). *A Change of Skies* likewise critiques exoticism and exoticist performances through its characters' embellishment of their "exotic" identities for personal gains (Veena's for peer approval, and Barry's for both female and media approval).

In the epilogue of *A Change of Skies*, Gooneratne presents exoticist identities as ambivalent concepts for diasporics – stereotypes which simultaneously attract and repel. She shows Veena's positive and negative reactions to exoticism, and specifically to the mechanics of exoticist naming (which relates to the focus on naming earlier in the novel, a thematic of all her novels). Whilst Veena happily uses exoticist naming to gain peer approval at university, she is clearly perturbed that those outside her peer group have exoticist assumptions of her. For instance, "the Golden Oldies" at Aunty Maureen and Uncle Bruce's Christmases try to position her within their telefilmic-influenced exoticist/colonialist nostalgia fantasies of South Asia, à la *The Jewel in the Crown*, by suggesting that her namesake was the last Vicereine of India, Lady Edwina Mountbatten (Gooneratne 1991, 116). Veena believes that she is above the allures of exoticism. She makes fun of Aunty Maureen's vision of Asia as "a world of Maharajas and marble palaces and magic carpets, an exotic fairytale in which even the beggars are picturesque" (318). She claims to wield a "detached, rational, [and] objective" gaze (315), knowing that "the magic's gone" and that "the beggars are crooks and conmen" (318). That she also admits nostalgia for a musical-themed Asian fairy tale, "The Tale of the Merchant's Daughter", as told to her by her mother, reflects her ambivalence toward the exotic (321).[3]

The epilogue also presents such ambivalence in Veena's diasporic experience through her attitudes to Sri Lanka and Sri Lankans. For instance, when reflecting on Australian newspaper headlines, "Tamil Tigers fighting for Jaffna [...] refugees [in Gulf states ...] 90,000 people from Sri Lanka", she tells herself that there is "no room for sentiment [...] you've got to look at the numbers. Look at it rationally, be objective. It's the figures that matter" (Gooneratne 1991, 315–325). This statement contradicts her previous thoughts on the "why" of this Sri Lankan refugee crisis, which is linked to colonial history in Veena's subsequent musings. She reflects on "the old Walauwa in Matara", which she might "check out" for her study on "Declining Economies of the Third World" (325). The comic vacillation of her thoughts through this monologue on economics past and present, together with her reflections on this particular Gulf state refugee crisis, indicates connections between the socio-economic realities of the past and the present for Sri Lankans and Sri Lanka. Moreover, this ambivalence elucidates Veena's own need to connect with the past, which she consistently denies, saying: "I'm not interested in the past, only in the present and the future, which is why I'm making this field trip" (317). The irony is palpable and relentless, reminding readers of Gooneratne's double-coded dialectic throughout the novel, which consistently critiques the postcolonial migrant condition.

Despite her arguments to the contrary, Veena's double-speak exposes her as an individual who is deeply influenced by the past and by the diasporic experience of her "mum and dad [who] had a hard time coming to terms with the changes [...] at home" (Gooneratne 1991, 320), her dad especially, who "[w]hen he wasn't thinking about 'home' [...] was writing about it" (321). Her story reflects the old idiom that "those who don't learn from the past are bound to repeat it", since it is clear that Veena, although denying the significance of the past, is nevertheless about to repeat the actions of her forbears (including her father, great-grandfather and mother) by journeying abroad and searching for meaning whilst carrying a notebook. In the context of Veena's second-generational status, this repetition of the self-reflexive journey shows the diasporic's search for meaning as having an intergenerational impetus, which illustrates Berg and Eckstein's (1991, 10) position on the intergeneration continuance of diaspora.

If the Moon Smiled (2000) and *Softly as I Leave You* (2011)

Chandani Lokugé is another Sri Lankan-Australian diaspora writer who is critically recognized for her representation of diaspora trauma and diasporic "double-consciousness" in fiction (Mukhopadhyay 2013; Paranjape 2002, 81–114; Watkins 2015, 165–207). Her approach, however, is entirely different to Gooneratne's – which, in spite of its critical commentary, ultimately celebrates the migrant condition (Watkins 2015, 166). Lokugé's strategy is indubitably more serious. Reading the diasporic condition through the lenses of trauma, mourning and melancholia, the model minority stereotype, and racism in Australia, she has written three immigration tragedies: *If the Moon Smiled* (Lokugé 2000), *Turtle Nest* (Lokugé 2008) and *Softly as I Leave You* (Lokugé 2011a). In my study, *Problematic Identities in Women's Fiction of the Sri Lankan Diaspora* (Watkins 2015 123–164, 165–207), I examined first-generation diasporic trauma, mourning, melancholia and schizophrenia in *If the Moon Smiled*. In what follows here, I will analyse Lokugé's representations of second-generation diaspora both in that novel and in *Softly as I Leave You*. Both feature children who are damaged by their parents' well-meaning over-involvement in their lives, which puts them on a path to disaster. In the first novel, it is a misguided father who causes the tragedy for the child protagonists, whereas in the second it is the mother. Lokugé frames the weight of parental expectation as a great burden for her teenage and young adult characters. The discussion will now consider the ways in which these novels critique the model minority stereotype and racism, respectively, in Australia.

Lokugé's first novel, *If the Moon Smiled,* presents shades of diaspora consciousness in each of its four first-generation diaspora characters. The novel's representation of second-generation diaspora consciousness is conveyed through its young adult characters, Devake and Nelum, Manthri's children, who represent the model minority stereotype as a gendered burden. Devake's story of father/son conflict is a critical parable of the model minority culture in Australia. Devake is harassed by his controlling father, Mahendra, for failing to meet the model minority benchmark of studiousness and high academic ability. Mahendra wants Devake to focus only on his studies in order to achieve high scores in his Matriculation (Year 12) and thereafter to study medicine at university. He forces Devake to study science and maths, for which he has no aptitude, and dismisses his interest in the arts and popular grunge culture. Disaster ensues, since Devake, unable to please his father, withdraws further into grunge culture, represented in the novel by the artist Kurt Cobain and his band Nirvana. He then starts smoking marijuana, fails his exams, becomes a drug addict and is permanently estranged from his family. This tragedy shows Mahendra as indoctrinated by the model minority stereotype. He expects his son to study medicine at university because it is esteemed among the Sri Lankan community, and is so intolerant of alternative possibilities that he terrorizes Devake, refusing to acknowledge his actual abilities and driving him to failure. The irony is that the more that Mahendra pushes his son to succeed and behave "appropriately", the more Devake turns the other way.

Mahendra's rejection of Devake's beloved grunge culture and music can be seen to articulate the age-old conflict between parents and children regarding popular culture; this takes on wider significance in the context of the family in diaspora in which tensions between parent, child and popular culture are also framed as between the "homeland" and host culture – in this case, Sri Lankan culture versus western influence. Such tension is ironic when, as Nelum states later, the family diaspora is a choice: "You brought us to Australia [she says]. We're not Sri Lankans any more" (Lokugé 2000a, 119). Mahendra defends his choices, and views his immigration as justification for the high, gendered expectations that he places upon on his children. He demands absolute control of Devake, dictating that

> I've sacrificed my whole life for you – my career, my country, only for you to have a good education. Go on now, go and study. You must not neglect your work for a single moment. Music? What music? What future with music, ah? Play in a band? Do you want the whole world to laugh at us? No, you're going to be a doctor. (73)

Mahendra's will is wounding, since although his children would like to please him, and indeed try to please him, they cannot fulfil his wishes.

Lokugé positions the model minority burden as indubitably gendered, and connected to Sinhalese Buddhist ideologies on gender – "duty […] caste […] religion [… and] race" (Lokugé 2000a, 103) – as shown through her juxtaposition of the predicaments of Devake and Nelum. On the one hand, the son, Devake, fails his father, Mahendra, because he lacks academic ability in maths and science, stereotypically masculine disciplines; on the other, Nelum fails Mahendra because, unlike her brother, she has a high level of academic ability, is ambitious and wants to become a surgeon. She successfully avoids disappointing

Mahendra during her school years because of her academic talents, but fully anticipates that "freedom must end with her degree" (119) because she is a girl. Mahendra expects her then to enter an arranged marriage after graduation, and subsequently to become a good Sinhalese-Buddhist wife to a "high caste, [and] high class" (167) Sri Lankan, an arrangement Nelum does not want, and from which she literally runs away when she flees her imminent wedding in Sri Lanka. Returning home to Australia, she shatters her father's expectations further by moving in with an Australian boyfriend, although the two break up soon after, as she pursues her career in a different city from him.[4] Thus for Nelum, as for Devake, Mahendra's effort to control the situation leads to a result that is fundamentally opposed to his own wishes. As is the case in the Devake storyline, this narrative outcome illustrates severe disconnections between the generations of this immigrant family, which challenge sociological readings of second-generation diasporics as being expert "cultural brokers" for their parents and community (Vasta 1993, 220; Houseknecht and Pankhurst 2000, 285).

Softly as I Leave You

Lokugé's (2011a) most recent novel, *Softly as I Leave You*, again presents the weight of parental expectations as unbearable, since seemingly it is the protagonist herself who leads her son to a premature death, despite having the best of intentions when acculturating him as a Sri Lankan. The trouble starts when her son Arjuna's involvement in a Sri Lankan charity group is misrepresented by the media as fundraising for terrorism in Sri Lanka. He is consequently targeted at a nightclub by thugs who effectively beat him to death when they recognize his "terrorist" identity. This story reflects the problematics of non-western acculturalization in western locations, the misrepresentation of terrorism by the Australian media and government, and the relationship of this to race-based hate crimes against non-western identities in Australia. The story seems to have been inspired by the Australian government and media's recent framing of Sri Lankan identities as terrorists. A prime example was the court case involving three Sri Lankans who were accused of terrorism in 2007 because of their support for a charity organization accused of directing funds into the Liberation Tigers of Tamil Eelam (LTTE). They were eventually released in 2010 on good behaviour bonds (Hagan 2010). Sri Lankan identities have also been vilified through the Tamil refugee crisis, which followed the cessation of the Sri Lankan Civil War. Newspaper headlines such as "Tamil Tigers at the Front Door", about "asylum seekers with links to Tamil terrorists", have proved sensational reading (Neighbour 2010). Lokugé's use in her plot of a vigilante "bashing" also seems to allude more generally to the culture of Islamophobia that has developed in Australia since 9/11, as critically manifested in the Cronulla Riots on Australia Day (January 26) in 2005 (see Julian 2015, 118). Although the protagonist's son is not Muslim (his mother is a Sinhalese Buddhist), the novel shows the way in which anti-terrorism hysteria like anti-Muslim sentiment in Australia, can (and has) supported violent hate crime. Furthermore, following government and community responses to Islamophobia, the narrative introduces questions about the right way to raise children in diaspora.

The novel suggests that Arjuna has been treacherously positioned in Australia since childhood by his immersion in Sri Lankan culture, and that his mother's fostering of his interests in Sinhala history and stories has led him to feel unduly connected to the situation in Sri Lanka. This has motivated his fundraising activity for the falsely accused "Metta Fund" charity, and then to his being wrongfully accused by the Australian media as a terrorist sympathizer/supporter (Lokugé 2011a, 39). The causal trajectory identified here makes a comment on the problematic nature of Australian multiculturalism. It implies that Australia, at least at the point in time when this story is set, reacts in a particularly volatile manner to allegations of terrorism, and is unconcerned with facts. The narrative suggests that interest in non-western cultures is a dangerous business for non-Anglo Australian young people and should be suppressed in favour of safer western options, due to the heated climate of xenophobia and the presence of thugs threatening to attack innocent victims at any moment. This damning portrait of the Australian zeitgeist in the new millennium undoubtedly critiques Australian realities. It reflects the negative framing of immigrant identities in Australia and the devolution of Australian multiculturalism policy since the Howard era, which has been permitted through the politics of counter-terrorism (Poynting 2008, 8).[5] Of this culture, it is worth noting the current resurgence of anti-immigrant politics in Australia and internationally, albeit post-dating Lokugé's novel. Recent examples include tough responses to the Syrian refugee crisis, characterized as an Islamic "invasion"; the "Brexit" fiasco, which generated a "surge in anti-immigrant hate crime"; the Donald Trump 2016 US presidential campaign, proposing the "extreme vetting of immigrants"; and the Australian Federal Election, which resulted in the re-election of the notorious anti-Islam senator, Pauline Hanson (One Nation party) plus three of her first-time elected party members ("This Racist Backlash against Refugees" 2016; Stone 2016; ABC News 2016). Hanson is one of several newly elected Australian senators who are reported as wanting to remove "section 18C from the 'Racial Discrimination Act' [which] makes it unlawful [in Australia] to publicly 'offend, insult, humiliate or intimidate another person or a group of people' on the basis of race" (Storming a Church in Muslim Garb the Latest Stunt of Party for Freedom's Nick Folkes 2016; see also "The Raging Debate on Section 18C" 2016).

Lokugé expounds her critique of racism in Australia through her protagonist Uma's ongoing reflections on her immigrant identity (her insecurity about her cultural difference from Anglo Australian friends, whom she suspects are racist), the Sri Lankan refugee crisis, and the positioning of her son Arjuna as a Tamil terrorist supporter (despite his being Sinhalese). Uma's concern reflects the clustering of the categories – immigrant, non-western "Other", refugee, and terrorist – by the Australian government and media, which has occurred in the Sri Lankan context and more generally since 9/11 (see McCulloch 2004, 89; Anderson and Taylor 2005, 464; Humphrey 2014, 83). As *Softly As I Leave You* indicates, the refugee "question" has become especially loaded and problematic for Australia's Sri Lankan community (Lokugé 2011a, 492). It has involved the afore-mentioned concerns of the Australian government and media about Tamil refugees with terrorist connections (Neighbour 2010). Also, it has involved the politics of inclusion/exclusion: the Australian government's stance on risk for Tamils in Sri Lanka, as well as their detention by the Australian government and attempted return to Sri Lanka (Human Rights Law Centre 2015). By reflecting on these issues in the lead-up to the "bashing" of Arjuna, Lokugé critiques the slippage of counterterrorism in Australia into refugee and immigrant issues. And, through the tragedy that ensues, she illustrates its heightened significance for second-generation diasporics.

In her article "Journey into Vishranti", Lokugé (2011b) considers the significance of Sri Lankan refugee issues for the wider Sri Lankan community in Australia. She presents her commentary through a conversation she has with a Sri Lankan woman at a Buddhist temple in the Blue Mountains, New South Wales. The woman, although missing her homeland, is philosophical about her struggle as an immigrant in Australia:

> "We are better off than those boat people. They'll be in detention camps for years. Worse than going to prison, isn't it?"

> It saddened me that she measured her situation against her compatriots who were in worse turmoil. Those "boat people" swindled by people smugglers. Among them victims of the war, opportunistic post-terrorists and poverty-stricken ordinary people. Those "Sri Lankan and Afghani boat people seeking asylum" […] unwanted baggage uncomfortably and indiscriminately dumped in detention centres (BBC News 2010). Among them, children screaming in nightmares […] stitching up their lips to gain government attention […]

> These are harrowing narratives that shadow my own. (Lokugé 2011b, 492)

Lokugé's grouping of "Sri Lankan and Afghani boat people" reflects the treatment of these groups as a collective unit by the Australian government and media, and their collective rejection by the Australian government, which occurred close to the publication of her article. *The Guardian* reported on April 9, 2010 that Australia had announced a suspension of new "refugees claims from Sri Lanka" and Afghanistan on the basis "that the situation [was] improved enough that [these groups] no longer need to seek protection elsewhere". As *The Guardian* observed, this "suspension of refugee claims" coincided with the government's struggle "to cope with an influx of boatloads of asylum seekers who […] filled an offshore detention centre and fuelled political debate over immigration policies" ("Australia Stops Accepting Refugee Claims from Sri Lanka and Afghanistan", 2010). Lokugé's caustic description of these unfortunate people as "opportunistic post-terrorists" recalls the aforementioned post-9/11 and post-Sri Lankan Civil War representations of asylum seekers by governments and the media as potential or retired terrorists.

In Lokugé's novel, the TV news headline "Terrorism in the 21st Century", reporting three millennial terrorist stories (one fictional and two real-world) – Arjuna's, that of bin Laden (the al-Qaeda leader) and that of David Hicks (the Australian convicted of supporting jihad but recently acquitted) – points readers again to Lokugé's critique of real-world terrorism issues and "terror" "beat-ups" by the media (Lokugé 2011a, 29; Bari Bari Atwan 2013, 24; Saul 2015, 13). Whilst the bin Laden story is *bona fide*, the David Hicks conviction has been proven invalid, and was being investigated at the time that Lokugé was writing this novel (Neighbour 2010). The David Hicks story thus symbolizes wrongful accusations of terrorism, and through Hicks's real-world incarceration and torture at Guantanamo Bay illustrates the calamities of terrorism hysteria, as manifested post-9/11 (ABC News 2015). Lokugé's critique of counterterrorism situates *Softly as I Leave You* within a reactionary body of literature, categorized as "post-9/11 fiction". This relatively recent category, including titles such as Richard Flanagan's *The Unknown Terrorist*, Mohsin Hamid's *The Reluctant Fundamentalist*, and Ian McEwan's (2005) *Saturday*, has developed since 2001 (Jones 2016, 63). As David Jones explains in "The Novel Response to Jihad", the novels that fall under this label often present the terrorist as a "fiction of the security state" (66). They encourage a sceptical and critical response to counterterrorism politics, as does Lokugé – although her approach is not so much concerned with conspiracy theory as with warning against the dangers of ill-informed media sensationalism, and reflection on the precarious nature of civil society.

Conclusion

The Sri Lankan diaspora novels discussed in this article portray second-generation diasporic characters as being "far more comfortable with bicultural identities" than first-generation diasporic characters, which hence supports current sociological theories on diaspora (Julian 2015, 113). They also suggest, however, that the significance of "homeland" trauma is great for second-generation immigrants. Indeed, there is a distinctive spillover of issues between the generations in these novels. The model minority stereotype and racism are shown to be especially important for characters in Lokugé's familial tragedies, and the weight of history is unavoidable in Gooneratne's satirical prose. The studies by Houseknecht and Pankhurst, and by Vasta, challenging the significance of the axiom of "caught between two cultures" for second-generation immigrants, is not substantiated by these texts, which show second-generation characters as negotiating the complications of their mixed cultural identities, albeit to varying degrees (Houseknecht and Pankhurst 2000, 284; Vasta 1993, 220).[6] This suggests that diaspora is a complicated business with a slide-on effect through generations. Additionally, if the themes in these novels are compared, as reflecting the evolution of multiculturalism politics from Gooneratne's (1991) *A Change of Skies* to Lokugé's (2011a) *Softly as I Leave You*, we could say that the problematics of the second-generation diaspora have, if anything, increased over time, since the concerns of Gooneratne's Veena are not life-shattering when compared with the second-generation problems in Lokugé's fiction. In large part, this is, of course, a result of the authors' different styles – comedy versus tragedy – although it can also be read as a reflection of the real-world increase in anti-immigration politics and anti-terror politics in Australia and globally since 9/11. It seems fitting here to end with the observations made by Wenche Ommundsen (2007) from "Multiculturalism Writing in Australia" that

> the paradoxical situation of contemporary Australia is that the population, and arguably its culture, has never been more multicultural, [also …] cultural diversity has wider popular appeal than ever before, but at the same time cultural and ethnic intolerance has gained a new "respectability" in political and public discourse. (80)

This analysis, although now nine years old, is disturbingly current. It has undoubted significance for the future of second- and subsequent-generation immigrants in Australia, and also for the direction of second-generation diaspora literature.

Notes

1. See Ommundsen (2007, 73–86) on the development of multicultural literature in the 1980s, and the subsequent backlash in the 1990s.
2. The "White Australia Policy", which discriminated against non-western immigrant identities, was only legally dismantled through the Racial Discrimination Act 1975. This Act prohibits discrimination "based on race, colour, descent or national or ethnic origin" by law (National Communications Branch: Department of Communications and Citizenship 2009).
3. Veena's attitudes also reflect what Robin Field (2004) describes, regarding Jhumpa Lahiri's work, as "the second generation's prerogative to alternatively pick and choose what elements of their cultural heritage to retain in their identities" (171).
4. Field, again speaking about Lahiri, says that "for second generational South Asian Americans, marriage is a fiercely contested aspect in this evolving culture. Indeed, the choice of a love marriage over an arranged match is one of the most important examples of the choice of one

particular cultural practice over another" (2004, 172). Lokugé's novel suggests that marriage is equally significant for Sri Lankans in Australia.

5. As Scott Poynting (2008) argues, there is a correlation between anti-terrorist laws, post-9/11, and racism in Australia. Poynting suggests that anti-terrorist laws were used to support the dismantling of multiculturalism policy in the first decade of the new millennium, and that this state sanctioning of racism has supported civil reactions to terrorism policy, including the Cronulla Riots of 2005.

6. As Salman Rushdie (1991) famously puts it, there are times "sometimes [when immigrants] "feel [as if they] straddle two cultures; at other times, [they] fall between two stools" (15).

Disclosure statement

No potential conflict of interest was reported by the author.

References

ABC News. 2015. "David Hicks: Former Guantanamo Bay Detainee, Foreign Fighter, Author." *ABC News*, January 23. http://www.abc.net.au/news/2015-01-23/david-hicks-profile/6032056.

ABC News. 2016. "Donald Trump Says He Would Implement 'Extreme Vetting' of Immigrants." *ABC News*, August 16. http://www.abc.net.au/news/2016-08-16/trump-says-he-would-implement-extreme-vetting-of-immigrants/7746500.

Akhter, A. F. M. Maswood. 2012. "Politics of Right to Write and Monica Ali's Fiction." *Asiatic* 6 (1): 95–12.

Anderson, Kay, and Affrica Taylor. 2005. "Exclusionary Politics and the Question of National Belonging: Australian Ethnicities in 'Multiscalar' Focus." *Ethnicities* 5 (4): 460–485. doi:10.1177/1468796805058095.

"Australia Stops Accepting Refugee Claims from Sri Lanka and Afghanistan." 2010. *The Guardian*, February 9. https://www.theguardian.com/world/2010/apr/09/australia-refugees-afghanistan-sri-lanka

Bari Atwan, Abdel. 2013. *After bin Laden: Al Qaeda, the Next Generation*. New York: The New Press.

Bhabha, Homi K. 1994. *The Location of Culture*. Abingdon: Routledge.

Brewster, Anne. 1995. *Literary Formations: Post-Colonialism, Nationalism, Globalism*. Carlton: Melbourne University Press.

Butler, Judith. 1993. *Bodies that Matter: On the Discursive Limits of 'Sex'*. Abingdon: Routledge.

Davis, Jessica Milner. 2009. "'Ethnic Comedy' in Contemporary Australia." *Australian Author* 41 (3): 20–2.

De Kretser, Michelle. 2016. "Interview with Alexandra Watkins on *Questions of Travel*." In *Journal of Postcolonial Writing* 52 (5): 568–576; reprinted in *South Asian Diasporic Women Writers: An Anthology of 21st Century Criticism*, edited by Ajay K Chaubey and Lisa Lau. Jaipur and New Delhi: Rawat Publications.

Eckstein, Susan, and Mette Louise Berg. 1991. "Introduction: Reimagining Migrant Generations." *Diaspora: A Journal of Transnational Studies* 18 (1/2): 1–23. doi: 10.1353/dsp.2015.0001.

Field, Robin. 2004. "Writing the Second Generation: Negotiating Cultural Borderlands in Jhumpa Lahiri's *Interpreter of Maladies* and *The Namesake*." *South Asian Review* 25 (2): 165–77.

Ganeshananthan, V. V. 2009. *Love Marriage*. New York: Random House.

Gooneratne, Yasmine. 1991. *A Change of Skies*. Sydney: Picador.

Gooneratne, Yasmine. 1996. *The Pleasures of Conquest*. Milsons Point: Vintage Australia.

Hagan, Kate. 2010. "Tamil Trio Accused of Terrorism Free on Bonds." *The Age*, April 1. http://www.theage.com.au/victoria/tamil-trio-accused-of-terrorism-free-on-bonds-20100331-revn.html.

Hamid, Mohsin. 2007. *The Reluctant Fundamentalist*. London: Penguin.

Harris, Anita. 2013. *Young People and Everyday Multiculturalism*. New York: Routledge.

Hartlep, Nicholas. 2015. *Modern Societal Impacts of the Model Minority Stereotype*. Hershey: Information Science Reference.

Houseknecht, Sharon K., and Jerry G. Pankhurst. 2000. *Family, Religion, and Social Change in Diverse Societies*. New York: Oxford University Press.

Human Rights Law Centre. 2015. "High Court Finds that Detention at Sea of 157 Tamil Asylum Seekers Was not a Breach of Australian Domestic Law." *Human Rights Law Centre*, January 28. http://hrlc.org.au/high-court-finds-that-detention-at-sea-of-157-tamil-asylum-seekers-was-not-a-breach-of-australian-domestic-law/.

Humphrey, Michael. 2014. "Securitization of Migration: an Australian Case Study of Global Trends." *Revista Latinoamericana de Estudios sobre Cuerpos, Emociones y Sociedad* 15 (6): 83–8.

Jones, David Martin. 2016. "The Novel Response to Jihad." *Quadrant* 60 (3): 63–8.

Joseph, Sarah. 2016. "Australia Found to Have Breached the Human Rights of David Hicks." *The Conversation*, February 22. https://theconversation.com/australia-found-to-have-breached-the-human-rights-of-david-hicks-55120.

Julian, Roberta. 2015. "Ethnicity and Immigrations: Changing the National Imaginary." In *Australian Sociology*, edited by David Holmes, Kate Hughes and Roberta Julian, 90–29. Melbourne: Pearson Australia.

Lee, Stacey. 2009. *Unravelling the Model Minority Stereotype*. New York: Teachers College Press.

Lokugé, Chandani. 2000a. *If the Moon Smiled*. Melbourne: Penguin Australia.

Lokugé, Chandani. 2000b. "'We Must Laugh at One Another, or Die': Yasmin Gooneratne's *A Change of Skies* and South Asian Migrant Identities." In *Shifting Continents/Colliding Cultures: Diaspora Writing of the Indian Subcontinent*, edited by Radhika Mohanram and Ralph J. Crane, 17–34. Amsterdam: Rodopi.

Lokugé, Chandani. 2008. *Turtle Nest*. Melbourne: Penguin Australia.

Lokugé, Chandani. 2011a. *Softly as I Leave You*. Melbourne: Arcadia.

Lokuge, Chandani. 2011. "Journey into Vishranti." *Interventions* 13 (3): 483–494. doi:10.1080/1369 801X.2011.597603.

McCulloch, Jude. 2004. "National (In)security Politics in Australia: Fear and the Federal Election." *Alternative Law Journal* 29 (2): 87–1.

McEwan, Ian. 2005. *Saturday*. London: Jonathan Cape.

Mukhopadhyay, Anway. 2013. "If the Moon Smiles on the Mappers of Madness: A Critique of the Cartographers of Insanity in Chandani Lokugé's *If the Moon Smiled*." *Transnational Literature* 5 (2). http://dspace.flinders.edu.au/jspui/bitstream/2328/26709/1/If_the_Moon_Smiles.pdf.

National Communications Branch: Department of Communications and Citizenship. 2009. *Fact Sheet 8: Abolition of the "White Australia" Policy*. Canberra: Australian Government Department of Immigration and Citizenship.

Neighbour, Sally. 2010. "Tamil Tigers at the Front Door." *The Australian*, July 16. http://www.theaustralian.com.au/national-affairs/tamil-tigers-at-the-front-door/story-fn59niix-1225892362845.

Ommundsen, Wenche. 2007. "Multicultural Writing in Australia." In *A Companion to Australian Literature Since 1900*, edited by Nicholas Birns and Rebecca McNeer, 73–86, Rochester, MN: Camden House.

Paranjape, Makarand. 2002. "Triple Ambivalence: Australia, Canada and South Asia in the Diasporic Imagination." *Australian Canadian Studies* 20: 81–13.

Poynting, Scott. 2008. "The Attack on 'Political Correctness': Islamophobia and the Erosion of Multiculturalism in Australia under the Howard Regime." *Social Alternatives* 27 (1): 5–9.

Puar, Jaspit, and Amir Rai. 2004. "The Remaking of a Model Minority: Perverse Projectiles Under the Spectre of Counter-Terrorism." *Social Text* 22 (3): 75–04. doi:10.1215/01642472-22-3_80-75.

Pung, Alice. 2008. *Growing Up Asian in Australia*. Melbourne: Black.

Richardson, Lizzie. 2015. "Theatrical Translations: The Performative Production of Diaspora." In *Dismantling Diasporas: Rethinking the Geographies of Diasporic Identity*, edited by Anastasia Christou and Elizabeth Mavroudi, 15–8. Abingdon: Routledge.

Rushdie, Salman. 1991. *Imaginary Homelands: Essays and Criticism, 1981–1991*. London: Granta Books.

Saran, Rupam. 2016. *Navigating Model Minority Stereotypes: Asian Indian Youth in South Asian Diaspora*. Abingdon: Routledge.

Saul, Ben. 2015. "Escape from Hell: A Spectacular Miscarriage of Justice." *Australian Book Review* 370: 13–4.

Stone, Jon. 2016. "Brexit: Surge in Anti-immigrant Hate Crime in Areas that Voted to Leave EU." *The Independent*, August 1. http://www.independent.co.uk/news/uk/crime/brexit-hate-crime-racism-immigration-eu-referendum-result-what-it-means-eurospectic-areas-a7165056.html.

"Storming a Church in Muslim Garb the Latest Stunt of Party for Freedom's Nick Folkes." 2016. *Sydney Morning Herald*, August 15. http://www.smh.com.au/federal-politics/political-news/storming-a-church-in-muslim-garb-the-latest-stunt-of-party-for-freedoms-nick-folkes-20160815-gqskrc

Tan, Carole. 2006. "The Tyranny of Appearance: Chinese Australian Identities and the Politics of Difference." *Journal of Intercultural Studies* 27 (1–2): 65–2. doi:10.1080/07256860600607660.

"The Raging Debate on Section 18C of the Racial Discrimination Act." 2016. *NITV SBS News*, August 15. http://www.sbs.com.au/nitv/nitv-news/article/2016/08/15/raging-debate- section-18c-racial-discrimination-act.

"This Racist Backlash against Refugees is the Real Crisis in Europe." 2016. *The Guardian*, February 25. https://www.theguardian.com/commentisfree/2016/feb/25/racist-backlash-against-refugees-greece-real-crisis-europe.

Vasta, Ellie. 1993. "Multiculturalism and Ethnic Identity: the Relationship between Racism and Resistance." *Journal of Sociology* 29 (2): 209–25. doi:10.1177/144078339302900204.

Watkins, Alexandra. 2015. *Problematic Identities in Women's Fiction of the Sri Lankan Diaspora*. Leiden: Brill.

Wu, Ellen. 2014. *The Color of Success: Asian Americans and the Origins of the Model Minority*. Princeton: Princeton University Press.

"The root of all evil"? Transnational cosmopolitanism in the fiction of Dewi Anggraeni, Simone Lazaroo and Merlinda Bobis

Paul Giffard-Foret

ABSTRACT

This article exposes the contradictions of cosmopolitan citizenship and world peace in novels by three Southeast Asian Australian women authors. Their fiction questions the viability of transnational sisterhood in an age of humanitarian intervention where women and children have become pawns for renewed western imperialist ventures. This article asks in turn whether the incommensurable space opened up by the failures of various forms of what Stuart Hall calls cosmopolitanism "from above" can be reinvested through "reading up the ladder of privilege", as proposed by Chandra T. Mohanty. Simone Lazaroo's *Sustenance* (2010) and Merlinda Bobis's *The Solemn Lantern Maker* (2008) build "grass-roots" forms of cosmopolitanism and touristic hospitality designed to redress the many evils of contemporary postcolonial societies. *The Root of all Evil* (1987) by Dewi Anggraeni objects to the Spivakian native informant and upwardly mobile migrant woman's imperious desire to help her homeland's subaltern female underclass, in light of the latter's lack of agency and the harm such intervention may cause.

[Plato's] pharmakon, this "medicine," this philter, which acts as both remedy and poison, already introduces itself into the body of the discourse with all its ambivalence. (Derrida 1981, 70)

The idea of cosmopolitanism circulates in academic circles with a steadfast popularity concomitant with the arrival of a "transnational turn". Chantal Zabus (2015) recently listed transnationalism, cosmopolitanism and utopianism as promising avenues for postcolonial studies. Cosmopolitanism's appeal owes a lot to the noble ideals it conveys: world peace and citizenship, cross-cultural understanding and "conversation" (Appiah 2006), internationalism and borderlessness. Yet as a number of critics point out (Brennan 1997; Gilroy 2005, 2013; Hall 2008), western imperialist ventures in the aftermath of 9/11 through the US's imposition of a new "Pax Americana", along with prolonged neo-liberal attacks on the commons, have cast suspicion upon the universalist and humanist premises of cosmopolitanism.

This article contributes to debates over the value of cosmopolitanism by highlighting its double-edged charge implied in the epigraph. Jacques Derrida's (1981) essay "Plato's Pharmacy" can be read as a criticism of Enlightenment philosopher Immanuel Kant's belief in the existence of an absolute moral law – the categorical imperative – on which Kant based his idea of cosmopolitan law. Kant's secularized version of Divine Intervention involved an obligation on the part of the powerful to help those less fortunate, despite the unfairness of the juridico-legal system and the barbarity of colonialism's civilizing mission. Whether "rooted" (Appiah 2005), "vernacular" (Bhabha 2000) or "from below" (Hall 2008), antinomic modes of cosmopolitan thought are articulated in order to make visible and to mediate the contradictions inherent in Kant's "pharmacy".

The trans*national* element in this article's title is of use in counterbalancing the anticipatory nature of a boundary-free and celestial-like *kosmos* inhabited by tranquilly coexisting peoples with more realistic, nation-bounded discourses (Spencer 2011, 4). Transnationalism captures this double bind between global interpenetration and the international division of labor that communism had thought of overcoming, through accenting how "historically, class has proved to be one of the most important sources of international solidarity" (Colas 1994, 530). This is not to dismiss the logic of an open-ended world free of chauvinism but to recognize the failures of top-down strategies emanating from political parties, multinational corporations, non-governmental organizations (NGOs) or supranational institutions. Thinking *trans*nationally also opens up transversal axes of solidarity across multiple sites of resistance and struggle "aimed at transcending the divided and unequal present" (Spencer 2011, 192).

Cosmopolitics, to be viable, must start from the vantage of the subaltern, rooted in "the particular standpoint of poor indigenous and Third World/South women" (Mohanty 2003a, 511). Chandra Mohanty's insights seem well suited to this article, not only because the literary texts it examines are written by Southeast Asian diasporic women of color. In fact, in refusing to embrace a limited use of identity and of gender racialized difference, Mohanty aims to develop a framework that "provides the most *inclusive* viewing of *systemic* power" (511; emphasis added) through the preservation of a cosmopolitan sense of social justice addressing *all* evils. The selected novels similarly engage conventions concerning diasporic identities as narrowly conceived by multiculturalism through being situated in Southeast Asia instead of Australia where its authors now live.

This gesturing outside the diasporic community and the Australian nation (Herrero, 2016) by the upwardly mobile migrant woman goes beyond the particulars of *ethnos* – that is, "one's *own* kind of people" – into a cosmopolitan literary space in translation/transaction with other minorities and with the homeland as *ethnikos* – that is, "*other* people, often taken to mean "heathen, pagan" (Spivak 2003, 83; emphasis in original). Cosmopolitan readers of postcolonial texts (Innes 2006) will grapple in the literary texts under analysis with marginalized personae including prostitutes, poor farmers or slum dwellers (*ethnikos*) coexisting with charitable do-gooders and philanthropists, foreign expatriates or tourists in search of an exotic piece of Nature (*ethnos*).

In dealing with the texts in an anticlockwise fashion, I operate a movement backwards to the *roots* of cosmopolitanism, and to the resurrection, from the Gulf War (1990–91) onwards, of the "evil" of humanitarian intervention. Simone Lazaroo's *Sustenance* (2010) and Merlinda Bobis's *The Solemn Lantern Maker* (2008) take subaltern women as a starting point "to access and make the workings of power visible – to read up the ladder of privilege" (Mohanty 2003a, 511). The bottom–top structure of these novels runs against the backdrop of the US-led global "War on Terror" and the microcosm of military outposts, tourist enclaves and shanty towns, to hint at makeshift forms of "subaltern hospitality" (Menozzi

2014, 159) incentivized by the reciprocated contingency of trauma and by basic survival needs such as food or shelter. Conversely, the earlier novel, *The Root of all Evil* by Dewi Anggraeni (1987), unravels the process through which a genuine concern for and sense of responsibility towards the oppressed by the native informant appears compromised when "shared above a class line that to some extent and unevenly cuts across race and the North-South divide" (Spivak 2004, 525). Postcolonial diasporics like Komala, the female protagonist in Anggraeni's novel, thus end up being unwitting agents of conservatism.

"Microcosm-opolitan" tourism in Simone Lazaroo's *Sustenance*

Sam Knowles (2007) has coined the term macrocosm-opolitanism "to emphasize the proliferation of meanings made to circulate around the original word" (2). Knowles bemoans the denaturation of cosmopolitanism that is a consequence of this proliferation, yet this fits the placelessness of those it purports to represent, such as international visitors, tourists or businessmen, when compared with "older", less mobile and more permanent types of migration. Of course, the flip side of this derivative tendency to travel (from *travail*: painful labor) is a growing dis-identification from society, and the formation of hedonism-driven transnational castes, cliques or clans – a phenomenon I call "microcosm-opolitanism".

Tourists in Lazaroo's novel *Sustenance* recreate at a microcosmic level and in a ludic way some of the key motifs of one's universe within a transplanted setting. The tourism industry's alleged aim of *dépaysement* (uprootedness) ends up stirring up the opposite by means of recolonizing the local landscape and its vital resources, including its inhabitants. The drawing of a parallel with colonialism may seem far-fetched, although not for Lazaroo. Her debut novel *The World Waiting to Be Made* (1994) describes the dying Christao (Malay-Portuguese) culture of her ancestors falling prey to the avid gaze of the western tourist. *The Australian Fiancé* (2000) and *The Travel Writer* (2006) feature western male expatriates with a keen photographic eye for the Orient, or writing articles for tour books like the *Lonely Planet*. As Huggan argues, the idea of the planetary "impl[ies] a broad-based cosmopolitan outlook on an increasingly interconnected but still politically and economically divided world" (2015, 141). When envisioned through the tourist globetrotter's eyes, planetarity can however remain as superficial as cosmopolitan renderings of diasporic belonging.

Nevertheless, outward differences exist between the tourist and the cosmopolitan, for the tourist does not claim to be a "citizen of the cosmos" beyond being a voyeuristic, transient presence. The tourist, unlike the cosmopolitan, does not participate directly in the colonial desire to pacify and purify the world, although new forms of environmentally friendly tourisms such as "green" or "eco" may do just this (Gilbert 2007). Tourists do not seek memories, only flavors in the form of cheap souvenirs; do not seek settlement, only counterfeited aftertastes of it. The tourist, especially en masse, makes a parody and mockery of the high-profile metropolitan cosmopolite's flirtatious courting of otherness. As Carrigan maintains, tourism represents "one of the rare occasions when privilege confronts poverty face to face" (2011, 151).

Endowed with the lofty goal of uniting people from different sociocultural backgrounds under the banner of planetary hospitality, tourism purportedly "results in positive changes in the attitudes of tourists towards the host culture contributing towards world peace" (Jafari 2000, 326). The trauma left in the wake of the Bali Bombings had the effect of making the War on Terror *heimlich* (homely) in an uncanny, melancholy way (Freud [1919] 1953; Gilroy

2005) for Australians flocking there for holidays. Amongst the 202 casualties, a disproportionate number (88) were Australian, followed by Indonesians (33). Reflecting the special place Bali occupies in the Australian imaginary, an Australian tourist in Lazaroo's novel muses over "the strange sadness she felt every time she left this island. *Like homesickness, really. But how can I be homesick for a place that was never mine?*" (2010, 273; emphasis in original).

Although not from Indonesia, Lazaroo demonstrates an intimate knowledge of Indonesia's geopolitical context and of the neocolonial nature of tourism in Bali. The touristic brochure from the aptly named Imperial Resort recalls the figure of the feudal/colonial landlord: "On the front page, bejewelled guests at the swim-up bar raised their glasses to farmers weeding the padi and to women bending their backs over their laundry in the river shallows *far below*" (Lazaroo 2010, 22; emphasis added). Instead of challenging the hierarchical structure of past colonial relations, the resort reproduces the illusion of a paradise overlooking/ looking over, yet cut off from, its surroundings so as to emulate feelings of "cocooning" (50) through total detachment.

While wanting to "relax", a guest at the hotel despairs that "one can't take a holiday in Bali any more without wondering if all the entrances to one's room are secured and guarded" (44). The terrorist menace alone does not explain the resort's bunker mentality and reluctance to let customers experience what lies beyond its gates. Tourists consume "staged" forms of authenticity (MacCannell 1973), seeking the "cooked" and a sense of the cultivated rather than the "raw". MacCannel distinguishes between "front" and "back", between the resort and its vicinity, adding how "it is always possible that what is taken to be entry into a back region is really entry into a front region that has been totally set up in advance for touristic visitation" (597).

This blurring means that Balinese villagers are given relative leeway to pass through the resort, thereby constituting an eyesore, and pushing a hotel guest to complain: "Why are the villagers allowed to wander through this resort? Not what you'd expect of a four-and-a-half-star hotel" (Lazaroo 2010, 56). As her partner rejoins, "Yeah, love. Some of them aren't exactly picturesque either, poor things" (56). The natives' assumed lack of hygiene thus needs to be removed for tourists to feel at home in the world. Home means that which is created out of one's image through dehumanizing and negating the other, instead of the "unhomely" (Bhabha 1992, 141) encounter between self and other.

Lazaroo reveals the falsity of a so-called host–guest relationship; in reality it is the host who is asked "to adapt to the presence of a foreign leisure class with different worldviews and expectations" (Freitag 1994, 545). So when villagers nearby ask hotel owners "for employment and compensation for loss of privacy", their requests are "met with silence" (Lazaroo 2010, 23). Moreover, the legendary Balinese congeniality turns out to be mythical, as the Balinese are in fact forced into acting to safeguard the tourism industry. A resort worker wonders "if Mrs Gloria or any of the other guests knew that orders to smile at the tourists appeared regularly in the local paper" (121). Another observes how "Balinese have to smile more than Westerners" (12).

How can one find cultural authenticity, if not through projecting on to others Arcadian fantasies of a place, pristine and virgin, waiting to be conquered, domesticated and *sanitized*? By hiding beneath the surface narratives of domination, exploitation, sexual abuse or terror (Carrigan 2011; Jaakson 2004; Watkins 2013), paradisal islands like Bali convert cosmopolitan ethics into a mere *cosmetic* gloss (Knowles 2007, 9). The recurring trope of *propreté* (cleanliness and its derivatives: property/propriety) must be read both as a purifying experience for the resort guests and as the product of racialized fears of pollution brought on by the possibility of the Other's intrusiveness: "*For now, light the aromatic oil burner. Cleanse and detox.* She [Clarissa Philips, a tourist from Perth] lowered herself into the Jacuzzi's rising water. What if it's contaminated?" (44; emphasis in original).

In the second half of the novel, a subaltern cosmopolitanism emerges. From mixed-race, Malaccan-English origins, the Elsewhere Hotel female cook Perpetua's fusion cuisine is used to defuse tensions between hostage-turned guests and terrorist-turned villagers/farmers from the neighboring island of Java. The name Perpetua brings to mind what Robert Spencer, drawing from Bohman and Lutz-Bachmann's version of cosmopolitanism, designates as "the Kantian ideal of hospitality and perpetual peace" (Spencer 2011, 24). At the same time, Perpetua's family history includes an absent English father regarded as "stateless" (Lazaroo 2010, 156), as well as a divorced Australian husband following the death of their child – yet "another abandoned [Malacca] Straits Settlements story that'll never be told in England" (9).

Perpetua's Lacanian lack of being is offset through whetting others' appetites, including Australian food critic Rex Broadfoot's, whose name implies an adventurous, wandering quality. Both characters use cooking and the "oral", for which "the mouth is the main source of pleasure and the centre of experience" (Stevenson 2010; 1248), as a metonymical substitute for the material constraints of belonging, and as compensation for failed relationships, as well as the loss of family. Yet in answer to Rex's business-cum-love proposal to follow him back to Sydney to work on a cookbook based on manufactured chemical ingredients like monosodium glutamate (MSG), a flavor enhancer believed to "have led to the extinction of hundreds of regional recipes in South-East Asia" (61), Perpetua cherishes a rootedness born from the memory of loss: "I haven't travelled or tasted as much of the world as you have. […] But I've learned this much, lah. It's best not to leave what we're sure we love" (Lazaroo 2010, 276).

The six starving young men responsible for holding hotel guests and staff hostage are also exiles – although not of their own volition. As they explain to Perpetua, Mr Wilson, the American owner of the Elsewhere Hotel,

> "visits our kampong and brings our brothers and sisters to stay with him here. He does this to them." The leader made a circle with his thumb and forefinger and moved his other index back and forth through the circle. (Lazaroo 2010, 226)

The hostage crisis concretizes the hotel's insularity and vulnerability to terrorism (as the guests become actual captives) while turning the tables. From being unwilling hosts to Mr Wilson's presence inside their home, the villagers become "unexpected guests" (*Sustenance*'s original title). Filippo Menozzi (2014) terms this form of postcolonial custodianship the "hospitality of the guest" (159).

At this point in the novel, physical force and unilateral talk replace the kind of cosmopolitanism envisaged by Kwame Anthony Appiah (2006), although the sense of impending doom helps bridge what French philosopher Jean-François Lyotard (1983) calls *différends* (phrases in dispute). As Perpetua notices when screening people's faces in the hotel's restaurant, "Easterners or Westerners, captors or hostages […] we are all reduced to the bones of our being" (Lazaroo 2010, 193). Communication harks back to the acts of eating and being fed that precede speech. While the Indonesian villagers and farmers are waiting for Mr Wilson's return, round-shaped dishes allegorizing a vision of "planetary conviviality"

(Spencer 2011, 4) are served to everyone – western captives thinking this is their last meal, the "thin, poverty-stricken" (Lazaroo 2010, 133) kidnappers enjoying their first feast: "When he [Jim Hopkins, an Australian tourist, himself a farmer] heard one of the captors belch appreciatively behind him, he felt he agreed with him" (216).

Perpetua's improvised deployment of culinary skills recalls Derrida's (2001) view of hospitality as governed not by invitation but by *visitation* (the appearance of a divine or supernatural being), and thus non-conditional and indeterminate a priori (22). Hospitality, according to Derrida, is also messianic, inspired by hope in the advent of radical alterity through cross-fertilizing contact. Perpetua's rejection of Rex's invitation to write a book shows it is the guest/reader, not the host/critic, who "make[s] the law" (*fait la loi*) in Derrida's words (2001, 14; emphasis in original), yet only insofar as such rules/recipes are seen as impermanent and subject to the transformative possibilities of self-othering processes: " 'Ah, the book. I'm not going to help you write it. I'm just going to...' She was making it up as she spoke, 'jot down my recipes for any guest who asks. And cook' " (Lazaroo 2010, 274).

Identity markers can be vectors of exploitation and/or emancipation. Food, especially, is marked by an imperious desire on the part of privileged subjectivities (men, colonists, capitalists) to *consummate* the essence of a culture. This was the experience of Perpetua's mother, Mercedes: "Forced by Oswald's departure to resume selling food from a makeshift stall, Mercedes stayed open late at night to capitalise on the hunger of the wealthier Malaccan men on their way home after satisfying other appetites at the brothels" (10). When conceived in a non-mercantilist way as sustenance (not consumption), sharing (not exchange), blessing (not supply), begging (not demand), food carries a quasi-spiritual dimension.

Unlike the cheap mysticism of some tourists for whom "Bali sorta takes the place of church and religion" (Lazaroo 2010, 34), Perpetua's Christian beliefs draw upon the Last Supper to enact a secularized cosmology from below, "as if heaven were being brought down to earth" (218). This cosmogony is in turn triggered by the illuminating materiality/meta-reality of death, and by hunger, "invok[ing] an originary or primordial Zuzage [commitment in German]" (Spivak 2012, 174) of the digestive system. In the words of a French tourist, "j'ai l'estomac dans les talons" (Lazaroo 2010, 231 232; my stomach is in my heels, or "I'm famished"). Having come as uninvited visitors to the mostly Australian-populated Elsewhere Hotel, Indonesian farmers return to their families with food galore. This visitation emphasizes community over universality, evoking early forms of regional commerce between indigenous Australia and Indonesia prior to European colonialism (Stephenson 2007, 22).

Urban cosmopolitics in Merlinda Bobis's *The Solemn Lantern Maker*

Supporters of globalization tout the concept of a global village (a single community linked by means of telecommunications) as a vision for the new millennium. While a significant portion of the world population owns mobile phones, many of these people have no roof above their head to call home. What remains of this utopian prophecy is the idea of (inter) dependency. Decisions made by food speculators in the US stock market have a direct impact on the livelihood of hundreds of thousands of farmers across the postcolonial world. When thrown off their land, these people subsist in mega-slums. Pace the idea of a cosmopolis united by belief in the bounties of trickle-down economics and free trade, these urban slums serve as a stark reminder that "issues of justice, citizenship and politics should now be conceptualized at the global scale" (Binnie 2006, 5).

In the Philippines, trade liberalization was supposed to integrate Filipino people into the world economy under the auspices of peaceful and equal partnership. Yet, according to Thornton, there is evidence that

[t]he Philippines lost hundreds of thousands of farming jobs after joining the WTO in 1995 [while] the plight of farmers fueled communist and Islamic resistance, especially on the island of Mindanao, home to more than two-thirds of the nation's corn production. (2008, 24)

Derrida's (2001, 4) notion of *cités-refuge* envisages the cosmopolis as a *ville franche* (open city) liberated from profit-driven motives and providing sanctuary for the victims of economic or climatic catastrophes like Typhoon Haiyan in late 2013. Third World megalopolises are *cités-refuge* par excellence, considering that most refugees are internally displaced. Noland, the child protagonist in Bobis's novel, along with his family, were made landless through concentration and cornering of land in the hands of agribusiness multinationals via the complicity of the Filipino state and a few big landowning families. In a fast-forwarded, short-circuited life on its way to premature adulthood, Noland witnessed the murder of his father, who "killed his landlord, hacked him to death [and] was shot while escaping" (Bobis 2008, 145).

A mute child made solemn by trauma, Noland and his alter ego Elvis are the literal embodiment of the Filipino people portrayed in Rudyard Kipling's ([1899] 1994) poem "The White Man's Burden" as "silent, sullen" and "half-devil and half-child" (334). Written in response to the American takeover of the Philippines following the Spanish-American War, Kipling's poem demands that America "veil the threat of terror and check the show of pride" (334). Despite the Philippines' gaining official independence from the US in 1946, US control of Filipino affairs continues uninterrupted – fostered by, amongst other things, the presumed threat of global communism (recoded as Islamism). This constitutes the historical backdrop of Bobis's novel, set in a post-9/11 climate of fear, with former Filipino President Arroyo vowing to combat homegrown terror.

After her husband's death, Noland's mother Nena has to relocate to the cosmopolitan anonymity of Manila with her son – since peri-urban stretches of land such as slums provide "an ideal hiding place" (Anderson 2007, 337). This *cité-refuge*/slum is also a *cité-refuse*, where "all the salvaged refuse of a city raised into homes, into lives leaning against each other" (Bobis 2008, 134). Unlike images of a harmoniously round-shaped globe – one and indivisible – Noland and his mother's hut alludes to the segregated world of *cités-dortoir* (dormitory towns) and *cités* (ghettoes) tout court: "It's a box, the poorest in the slums. It's scraps of corrugated iron, wood, cardboard and plastic, and a hole for a door, set apart from the rest of the huts, because here's where all the sewage flows" (5).

The slum is home to those left out of globalization: orphans like Noland's friend Elvis, or unwanted women like Cate Burns. The two little boys rescue Ms Burns, an American tourist, after she is caught in a street crossfire leading to the murder of a Filipino reporter. In privileging the terrorist plot, the Filipino government, under the active tutelage of the US military, aims to shift the blame onto resistance groups from the southern island of Mindanao following previous American hostage crises in this region: "The Philippine president commiserates with the American ambassador, emphasizing the friendship between the two countries. […] There's protest against America meddling with Philippine affairs, besides this is civilian matter, or are we seeing the usual neo-colonialism?" (Bobis 2008, 119).

That two native boys are responsible for the "kidnapping" of Ms Burns in a country referred to as "America's boy" by former US president Lyndon B. Johnson overturns paternalistic imperialist rhetoric of "white men saving brown women from brown men" (Spivak 1994, 93). Those women are often used as political pawns, since "additional legitimation for interminable war is discovered in the idea of humanitarian intervention and especially in the liberation of women, homosexuals and other vulnerable groups from the medieval claws of Islamist barbarism" (Gilroy 2013, 117–118). Under the pretext of fighting terrorist cells, the Filipino government, with the assistance of the US military, goes so far as to threaten to bulldoze down the slum where the American tourist is kept hidden while recovering.

The slum illustrates environmental racism, functioning within a genocidal ecology of cleansing. Clearing it up will likely allow for more foreign investment and land grabbing. The documenting of 6,000 families threatened with internal displacement into a far-off area subject to flooding and earthquake as a result of the new Quezon City CBD plan (Revelli 2012) sheds light on the social significance of urban and agribusiness development which displaces local populations twice: first from the countryside, then from inner city slums. Seen as "nothing people" (Bobis 2008, 125), slum dwellers must be eradicated in order for the Filipino government to present an uncorrupted image to the world. As a slum dweller haplessly comments: "Beat, rinse, wring, beat, rinse, wring. And flush down the city drain. This is what they'll do to us. It happens. They'll clean us up" (112).

Pushpa Agnihotri (1994) describes the slums of Madhya Pradesh in India as being of a "cosmopolitan nature", with "in-migrants from all states of the country" (90). Also coming from various provinces of the Philippines, the slum dwellers in *The Solemn Lantern Maker* are to be superseded by more glamorous, equally stateless cosmopolites for whom the *polis* amounts to a shopping mall, and citizenship according to a credit card number. Like the Quezon City CBD project, aspiring to become the biggest financial hub in the country, Manila's Glorietta Mall, where Noland is taken amid the Christmas frenzy with his friend Elvis, is located in the "shopping heart of the city" (Bobis 2008, 58). The mall represents a miniature world of opulence where money and goods circulate with disconcerting speed, so that "the choices will make you dizzy, the corridors will get you confused, get you lost" (59). Rich and poor alike set out on an expedition to be bathed in the "fake glory" of international brands in this heavenly place where "ignorance is bliss" (61).

The *cité-refuge*/slum is a place of oblivion, too, where individual lives have been crushed to silence by the imperative to survive. The silence surrounding Nena's husband's murder, Cate Burns's miscarriage or Elvis's earnings as a child prostitute in fancy hotels means communication must take place either at the ground level of "gossip" (Bobis 2008, 36) or within the heartfelt realm of "cosmic" dreams, rather than through language proper:

> The boy sketches the unknowable in his head, extending his comic strip from before, revising the cosmic. Four stars in the sky. Big angel falling from the fourth star. Small angel flying from the first star. Small angel on the pavement, arms open and waiting for the fall. (42)

Noland's fascination with angels and selling of *parols* as a hawker symbolically convey his muteness. A *parol* is a five-point star-shaped Christmas lantern and a traditional Christian decoration in the Philippines. It is also *parole* (speech). Made from a constellation of fallen signifiers/angels/comets, Noland's stream of consciousness runs counter to the preordained structural fixity of *langue* (language). It suggests an as yet unbreakable faith in the possibility of the quartet's (Noland/Nena/Elvis/Cate) forever criss-crossing destinies, and in the existence of a fifth Invisible Hand: the merciful, redemptive God Father. The ability to converse and commiserate is here a mut(e)ability:

'May alam akong kuwento…'	'I know a story….'
'So do I…'	'Ako rin…'
'Kuwentong di mo alam…'	'a story you don't know…'
'Nor do you know mine.'	'Di mo rin alam ang akin.' (42)

United by common grief, Cate and Nena understand one another although they do not speak the same language. This cosmopolitanism of the "wretched" successively applies to Cate, Elvis or US Colonel David Lane, a morally ruined man following military debacles in Afghanistan and Iraq. Mutual bonding is here made possible by lives freely intersecting and parting (instead of vertically and indefinitely imposed onto) one another:

> Nena stares into the blue eyes welling with tears. Her own fill too; the tug of grief runs between them, and much more. Pasts so estranged and futures that will never touch again. But here, they are irrevocably bound. Perhaps this is something they know but must deny so they can let the other go. (Bobis 2008, 134)

Upward mobility in Dewi Anggraeni's *The Root of All Evil*

Dewi Anggraeni's debut novel *The Root of All Evil* (1987) differs from the fiction previously discussed. Its central character, Komala, is a fulfilled, free-willed married woman with an international writing career, reflected in her choice of pen name. Unlike "Tanti Komalasari", the culturally unmarked "Laila Minogue", by sounding "more pronounceable and less foreign" (Anggraeni 1987, 37), gives Komala an entrée to the Australian literary scene. Komala is also a relatively well-known writer in her homeland Indonesia and throughout the world republic of letters, made up of academics and artists, but also philistine businessmen like Sonny, and bourgeois romantics like Hanny. Frequent allusions to cosmopolitan city locations such as Melbourne, Paris or Manhattan indicate that Komala is well traveled, while her Christian beliefs in a predominantly Muslim country lead one to think of a schooling in the Dutch tradition of the former colonizer, besides her Sundanese (Javanese) upbringing.

The novel's denouement, unfolding from Komala's quest to seek justice on behalf of the downtrodden of her homeland, will put into perspective the "celebratory", "skeptical" and "socialist" strands of cosmopolitanism (Spencer 2011). The socialist strand, in particular, analyzes "the role of economic factors in organizing 'humanity' in a hierarchical scale of class differences" (Braidotti, Hanafin, and Blaagaard 2013, 3). Learning of her father's stroke, Komala leaves behind the well-off outer suburbs in the Dandenong Hills in Melbourne, where she now lives, to return to Jakarta to look after him. Once a government clerk, her father, in his newfound dependency, allegorizes the passing of power between two types of native informant: "the descendants of the colonial subject" and "the new diasporic" (Spivak 2004, 525).

When boarding the plane for Jakarta, Komala is associated with, and travels alongside, men and women holding liberal professions in banking or information technology (her husband, Drew, is a doctor). Tom Nairn (2000) has dubbed this painless, reckless frequency with which such professionals are able to move freely across borders, airports and cities "departure lounge internationalism" (148). At the airport, Komala joins "the fastest moving queue" (Anggraeni 1987, 6); her experience of customs stands in sharp contrast to asylum seekers making the opposite journey, and being held in indefinite detention: "The customs officials just waved me past. I was totally unprepared for this, having expected to have my bags opened at least" (7).

Back in Jakarta after nine years, Komala bears witness to the ravages caused by disorderly urban development, gross inequalities and corruption at all levels. The opening up of the Indonesian market to the world economy has resulted in another transition, from the old bourgeoisie to the arriviste nouveau riche, besides that from old to new native informant. "As Jakartan business expanded, the residents, many of them established families with ever decreasing wealth […] had had to sell or lease their mansions to commercial enterprises" (Anggraeni 1987, 124). Sociocultural demarcations are not clear-cut, however. Komala's former lover Hanny manages to reinvent himself as an entrepreneur, meanwhile keeping an aristocratic distance from the likes of Komala's best friend Narsih's husband Nelson, "the badminton champion, the handsome son of Oscar Harahap, one of the richest men in Jakarta" (22).

As for Komala, she resembles a cosmopolitan *arrivé*, parachuted back to Indonesia and entering her home like a foreigner. While her outsider position disputes diasporic narratives of smooth, happy homecoming, Komala's feeling of ostracism arises from discovering that her parents have been forced to rent parts of their house to boarders. When she observes that her father could have benefited from a retirement pension if he were in Australia, he reminds her that to be live off welfare is not part of the Indonesian mindset. Such values clash with the Australian way of life she has grown accustomed to: "Was I becoming a foreigner in my own country? Had my sense of values changed?" (Anggraeni 1987, 88).

The egalitarianism of Australian society may explain Komala's defense of Tati and her brother Hamdani, a boarder at Komala's house. Komala's spontaneous and unquestioning feeling of empathy for Tati's fate gets articulated through the language of human rights, moral obligation and religious love. While seeking assistance from a legal aid agency, Komala must reckon with the reality of Jakarta's dog-eat-dog mentality, which makes it considerably harder for class, gender or faith-based solidarities to develop, in comparison with Australia. Women's dependency on men means they prefer to blame other women for their husbands' infidelities. Thus Tati was punished with sulphuric acid thrown at her face by the nightclub boss's wife for hoping to gain more status as his favored hostess than that of a kept woman.

Tati's defilement ignites in Komala a savior's duty, along with a specifically postcolonial representational burden towards the subaltern's right to humanity. As Spivak has argued, "the idea of human rights […] may carry within itself the agenda of a kind of social Darwinism – the fittest must shoulder the burden of righting the wrongs of the unfit" (2004, 524). Because of the ethical ground underpinning such discourse, the human rights advocate, as Ashcroft (2010) remarks, in effect "constructs cosmopolitanism as an attitude of mind rather than a subject position" (76). In doing so, Komala fails to see its paternalistic and deeply racist undertones. Asked if white men are better than "our men", Komala opts first for a diplomatic answer, yet, pushed by her interlocutor, concedes how "in general they're more considerate toward women" (Anggraeni 1987, 31). She plays here on orientalist tropes of submissive women, Asian despots and sexual predators, of which Tati's impotent brother Hamdani is the opposite.

Until Komala decides to help Tati, no one is willing to, and not only because Tati is a prostitute whose second-class status cheapens the value-worth of other women as commodities in the matrimonial market (as low-paid migrant work does in the labor market). Described by many as ambitious, Tati also commits the graver sin of rising above her status by working up through Jakarta's pyramidal structure. In the course of undertaking the "uphill job" (Anggraeni 1987, 94) of helping Tati and her brother, Komala admits her own feelings of inadequacy and impropriety. Her indecisiveness about prying and probing into another's life (24, 28, 31) or in positing herself as arbiter (72, 75) shows an awareness of her own subject position, yet she does not think of consulting Tati until too late: "It was all right for me. I was comfortably off, and did not have to worry about a sister agonising and fighting death. How dared I say 'we' when he [Hamdani] and I were on *completely different planes*?" (84; emphasis added).

The Root of All Evil asks what value can be wagered on a cosmopolitan ethics split across geo-economic lines of flight that may never cross each other. Spivak's attempt to rework Marx's concept of use-value "must account for the contemporary international division of labour and the economic dependency of many nations in the global south on global financial institutions such as the World Bank or the International Monetary Fund" (Morton 2007, 73). Faced with an economically depraved/deprived country, use-value (putting oneself to good use, as Komala does in trying to right wrongs) may prove useless or even abusive. As Isti, another prostitute at the nightclub, referring to her boss and the likes of him, explains: "You see, it's like a little kingdom where we work. He's one of the princes, we're only his peasants. They can do anything, my dear. We have to know our place" (Anggraeni 1987, 88).

The story of Endanang, the servant of Komala's relative Sinta, is telling. However common in Indonesia, owning a servant remains a sign of wealth, power and privilege. Endanang was sacked for failing to perform household chores after Komala attempted to improve her lot through inculcating in her liberal ideas of fraternity and equality. Despite defying norms of conduct and subverting master–servant relationships, Komala ends up "identifying with the comfortable middle-class and justifying Sinta's action" (Anggraeni 1987, 111). In Anggraeni's novel, foreign aid appears always already poisoned by the reality of precariousness, exploitation and the possibility of losing face. Maimed for life, Tati ultimately refuses Komala's help in seeking legal redress, for fear of bad publicity, while the other hostesses at Tati's nightclub are unwilling to testify in court.

To many, Komala's liberal cosmopolitan world view looks naive or idealistic, stemming from a misplaced sense of righteousness, pity or guilt leading her to overstep her position and "be pushy, thus disconcerting the people assisting as well as those assisted" (Anggraeni 1987, 127). Komala does not abandon her tendency to romanticize others' lives; her metaphorical fall from grace occurs after her father, considered a role model, dies having disclosed to her the secret of his own infidelities. Like a military occupying force, Komala feels reluctant to withdraw and let others take charge of Tati's case upon returning to Australia, but adds: "What right did I have to think that it would not proceed properly without me?" (128) Her confession to Hamdani sounds very much like an avowal of defeat: "I thought I understood the sufferings of the downtrodden women in this country. I thought I was enlightening people on the plight of others!" (137).

According to Spivak, "the most frightening thing about imperialism, its long-term toxic effect, what secures it, what cements it, is the benevolent self-representation of the imperialist as savior" (2012, 166). While indulging in self-criticism, as Komala does, seems disabling, perhaps to relinquish one's privileged positioning is what is needed. Stephanus, for example, after realizing "there's very little fair play in the world, especially in politics" (Anggraeni 1987, 116), dropped out of his academic studies in social and political sciences and went through the humbling experience of being a nightclub chauffeur at Tati's place of work. The owner,

Sonny Sudradjat, is described as a "distant relative" (115) of Stephanus. Unlike Stephanus, Sonny is "self-made"; unschooled and from a poor background, he managed to use his business acumen to erect a small empire in the entertainment and tourism hotel industries. While Stephanus may be a true cosmopolitan renegade in agreeing to testify in court, his motive for doing so suggests a freedom of choice (in upward and downward mobility alike) and a control over his destiny which a "country girl" (53) and widowed mother like Tati could never have dreamt of: "Because, when I took up this job, I knew I wouldn't be doing it forever. I'm young, I'm single. I can get by without a job for a while" (114).

Komala also hoped to reverse the pattern of dependency between Tati and herself. Her indiscriminateness at the men's club in a scene preceding Tati's aggression seemingly transgresses the line between prostitute and married wife, yet her call for help may also express a vicarious desire to *feel* for Tati, rather than a genuine sense of distress at being preyed upon:

> We [Komala and a client] were dancing closer and closer toward Tati and Baldy [Sonny's nickname]. When we were within winking distance, Tati saw me and looked rather surprised. Suddenly, in my desperate state, I concentrated on my facial muscles and tried to relay a "Help me!" message to Tati. To my great relief, Tati's eyes glistened with comprehension and she nodded very slightly. When we returned to our table, I started to doubt that I had really seen Tati's reply. (Anggraeni 1987, 59)

Conclusion

The title of Anggraeni's novel is a biblical reference derived from Timothy: "For the love of money is a root of all *kinds of* evil, for which some have strayed from the faith in their greediness, and pierced themselves through with many sorrows" (emphasis in original). In the face of power and greed, Komala's "Feminism Without Borders", taking the form of legal aid and humanitarian intervention, seems both a remedy and a poison, like Plato's Pharmacy. In particular, this (con)descending cosmopolitanism can potentially backfire in a context of recolonization of the Global South following the privatization and restructuring of Third World economies.

The other side of aid is debt. Masquerading as hospitality, rescue packages offered by the creditors of the International Monetary Fund or the World Bank have proven to be conditional, self-interested and apocalyptic, bringing forth the destruction of whole sections of the economy (from Greek *oikonomia*, "household management"). Of course, small-l liberals like Komala are themselves but pawns in empire's Great Game. So is Cate Burns, the American tourist in Bobis's novel, her disappearance serving as a cover-up in a country with one of the highest rates in the world for the assassination of journalists.

At the same time, Anggraeni's, Bobis's and Lazaroo's novels elaborate (in the sense of being produced by effort of labor) on the possibility of subaltern cosmopolitanisms anchored in "raced, and class communities of women from poor countries as they are constituted as workers in sexual, domestic, and service industries; as prisoners; and as household managers and nurturers" (Mohanty 2003b, 246). Mohanty has further made the case that

> [i]f we pay attention to and think from the space of some of the most disenfranchised communities of women in the world, we are most likely to envision a just and democratic society capable of treating all its citizens fairly. Conversely, if we begin our analysis from, and limit it to, the space of privileged communities, our visions of justice are more likely to be exclusionary because privilege nurtures blindness to those without the same privileges. (2003a, 510)

Answering the question of whether or not the idea of cosmopolitanism in the abstract is "evil" thus depends on subject positioning. In other words, cosmopolitanism's ambivalence is not absolute but relative to concrete forces at play.

Unlike Komala, western tourists in Bobis's and Lazaroo's novels feel compelled by the sheer drama of their predicament to confront the subaltern – and, in so doing, to give her agency. In that light, could a form of tourism be re-imagined "that counteracts exploitative colonial and commercial designs upon it, and that offers the opportunity to see it as a planetary (cosmopolitan) and/or postcolonial (autonomous) space?" (Huggan 2015, 140). Besides, tourism, terrorism, sex trafficking, religion or environment/urbanization-related issues transpiring from the novels are of ever-greater significance for postcolonial studies. These issues suggest that there is no root – but rather a rhizome – of evils. While a detailed study of each issue lies beyond the scope of this article, rewriting tourism as other-worldly encounter and as indigenized visitation makes for a starting point.

Disclosure statement

No potential conflict of interest was reported by the author.

References

Agnihotri, Pushpa. 1994. *Poverty Amidst Prosperity: Survey of Slums*. New Delhi: M.D. Publications.
Anderson Neil. 2007. *The Urban Community: A World Perspective*. New York: Routledge.
Anggraeni, Dewi. 1987. *The Root of All Evil*. Melbourne: Indra Publishing.
Appiah, Kwame A. 2005. "Rooted Cosmopolitanism." In *The Ethics of Identity*, 213–272. Princeton, NJ: Princeton University Press.
Appiah, Kwame A. 2006. *Cosmopolitanism: Ethics in a World of Strangers*. New York: Norton.
Ashcroft, Bill. 2010. "Transnation." In *Rerouting the Postcolonial: New Directions for the New Millenium*, edited by Janet Wilson, Cristina Sandru, and Sarah Lawson Welsh, 72–85. New York: Routledge.
Bhabha, Homi K. 1992. "The World and the Home." *Social Text* 31 (31/32): 141–153.
Bhabha, Homi K. 2000. "The Vernacular Cosmopolitan." In *Voices of the Crossing: The Impact of Britain on Writers from Asia, the Caribbean, and Africa*, edited by Ferdinand Dennis, and Naseem Khan, 133–142. London: Serpent's Tail.
Binnie, John. 2006. *Cosmopolitan Urbanism*. New York: Routledge.
Bobis, Merlinda. 2008. *The Solemn Lantern Maker*. Sydney: Pier 9.
Braidotti, Rosie, Patrick Hanafin, and Bolette Blaagaard, eds. 2013. *After Cosmopolitanism*. Abingdon: Routledge.
Brennan, Timothy. 1997. *At Home in the World: Cosmopolitanism Now*. Cambridge, MA: Harvard University Press.
Carrigan, Anthony. 2011. *Postcolonial Tourism: Literature, Culture, and Environment*. New York: Routledge.

Colas, Alejandro. 1994. "Putting Cosmopolitanism into Practice: the Case of Socialist Internationalism." *Millennium - Journal of International Studies* 23 (3): 513–534.

Derrida, Jacques. 1981. *Dissemination*. Chicago: Chicago University Press.

Derrida, Jacques. 2001. *On Cosmopolitanism and Forgiveness*. London: Routledge.

Freitag, Tilman G. 1994. "Enclave Tourism Development: For Whom the Benefits Roll?" *Annals of Tourism Research* 21 (3): 538–554.

Freud, Sigmund. [1919] 1953. "The Uncanny." In *The Standard Edition of the Complete Psychological Works of Sigmund Freud*, 217–256. vol. XVII, London: Hogarth Press.

Gilbert, Helen. 2007. "Ecotourism: A Colonial Legacy?" In *Five Emus to the King of Siam: Environment and Empire*, edited by Helen Tiffin, 51–70. Amsterdam: Rodopi Press.

Gilroy, Paul. 2005. *Postcolonial Melancholia*. New York: Columbia University Press.

Gilroy, Paul. 2013. "Postcolonialism and Cosmopolitanism: Toward a Worldly Understanding of Fascism and Europe's Colonial Crimes." In *After Cosmopolitanism*, edited by Rosi Braidotti, Patrick Hanafin, and Bolette Blaagaard, 111–131. New York: Routledge.

Hall, Stuart. 2008. "Cosmopolitanism. Globalisation and Diaspora: Stuart Hall in Conversation with Pnina Werbner." In *Anthropology and the New Cosmopolitanism: Rooted, Feminist and Vernacular Perspectives*, edited by Pnina Werbner, 345–360. Oxford: Berg Publishers. .

Herrero, Dolores. 2016. "Merlinda Bobis's *Fish-Hair Woman*: Showcasing Asian-Australianness, Putting the Question of Justice in its Place." *Journal of Postcolonial Writing* 52 (5): 606–617.

Huggan, Graham. 2015. "Notes on the Postcolonial Arctic." In *The Future of Postcolonial Studies*, edited by Chantal Zabus, 130–143. New York: Routledge.

Innes, C. Lyn. 2006. "Cosmopolitan Readers and Postcolonial Identities." In *Global Fissures: Postcolonial Fusions*, edited by Janet Wilson, and Clara A.B. Joseph, 171–184. Amsterdam: Rodopi Press.

Jaakson, Reiner. 2004. "Globalisation and Neocolonialist Tourism." In *Tourism and Postcolonialism: Contested Discourses, Identities and Representations*, edited by Michael Hall Collin, and Hazel Tucker, 169–183. New York: Routledge.

Jafari, Jafar. 2000. *Encyclopedia of Tourism*. New York: Routledge.

Kipling, Rudyard. [1899] 1994. "The White Man's Burden." In *The Collected Poems of Rudyard Kipling*, 334–345. Hertfordshire: Wordsworth Editions.

Knowles, Sam. 2007. "Macrocosm-opolitanism? Gilroy, Appiah, and Bhabha: The Unsettling Generality of Cosmopolitan Ideas." *Postcolonial Text* 3 (4): 1–11. http://postcolonial.org/index.php/pct/article/viewFile/731/497

Lazaroo, Simone. 2010. *Sustenance*. Crawley, Western Australia: UWA Publishing.

Lyotard, Jean-François. 1983. *The Differend: Phrases in Dispute*. Translated by Georges Van Den Abbeele. Minneapolis, MN: University of Minnesota Press.

MacCannell, Dean. 1973. "Staged Authenticity: Arrangements of Social Space in Tourist Settings." *American Journal of Sociology* 79 (3): 589–603.

Menozzi, Filippo. 2014. *Postcolonial Custodianship: Cultural and Literary Inheritance*. New York: Routledge.

Mohanty, Chandra T. 2003a. "'Under Western Eyes' Revisited: Feminist Solidarity Through Anticapitalist Struggles." *Signs* 28 (2): 499–535.

Mohanty, Chandra T. 2003b. *Feminism without Borders: Decolonizing Theory, Practicing Solidarity*. Durham, NC: Duke University Press.

Morton, Stephen. 2007. *Gayatri Spivak: Ethics, Subalternity and the Critique of Postcolonial Reason*. Cambridge: Polity Press.

Nairn, Tom. 2000. *After Britain: New Labour and the Return of Scotland*. London: Granta.

Nelson, Thomas. 1982. *The Holy Bible: New King James Version*. Nashville, TN: Nelson Publishing.

Revelli, Philippe. 2012. "D'abord, ils ont pris ma Terre[First, they took my Land]." June 1. Documentary Photography. Accessed 8 June 2016. http://philipperevelli.com/?p=1308

Spencer, Robert. 2011. *Cosmopolitan Criticism and Postcolonial Literature*. New York: Palgrave Macmillan.

Spivak, Gayatri C. 1994. "Can the Subaltern Speak?" In *Colonial Discourse and Post-Colonial Theory*, edited by Patrick Williams, and Laura Chrisman, 66–111. Hertfordshire: Harvester Wheatsheaf.

Spivak, Gayatri C. 2003. *Death of a Discipline*. New York: Columbia University Press.

Spivak, Gayatri C. 2004. "Righting Wrongs." *The South Atlantic Quarterly* 103 (2-3): 523–581.

Spivak, Gayatri C. 2012. *An Aesthetic Education in the Era of Globalization*. Cambridge, MA: Harvard University Press.

Stephenson, Peta. 2007. *The Outsiders Within: Telling Australia's Indigenous-Asian Story*. Sydney: University of New South Wales Press.

Stevenson, Angus, ed. 2010. *Oxford Dictionary of English*. 3rd ed. Oxford: Oxford University Press.

Thornton, Songok H. 2008. "People Power and Neocolonial Globalism in the Philippines." *Asia Journal of Global Studies* 2 (2): 20–34.

Watkins, Alexandra Elizabeth. 2013. "Babes in the Sand and Flying Predators: Touristic Corruption, Exoticism and Neocolonialism in Chandani Lokugé's *Turtle Nest*." *Postcolonial Text* 8 (2): 1–19. http://postcolonial.org/index.php/pct/article/view/1618/1538

Zabus, Chantal. 2015. "Introduction: The Future of Postcolonial Studies." In *The Future of Postcolonial Studies*, edited by Chantal Zabus, 1–15. New York: Routledge.

Merlinda Bobis's *Fish-Hair Woman*: Showcasing Asian Australianness, putting the question of justice in its place*

Dolores Herrero

ABSTRACT

Fish-Hair Woman took 17 years to write and was rejected by six publishers – the "gatekeepers" of the Australian publishing industry, according to Bobis. One of main problems when trying to locate the novel as Asian Australian is that it is set in a militarized village in the Philippines, and therefore Australia and the Australian story occupy only a marginal position. This article will study the novel's attempt to dilute and reverse this centrality by immersing white Australian characters in foreign and dangerous Asian settings. Some theories put forward by trauma and memory studies will also be used to show how *Fish-Hair Woman* manages to dig up individual traumatic memories from their ruins so that the painful collective past can somehow be reconstructed and brought to the surface, the memory of the disappeared can finally be honoured, and resilience can pave the way for hope in a better future.

In her essay "Voice-Niche-Brand: Marketing Asian-Australianness", Merlinda Bobis (2008) adamantly claimed that so-called "ethnic" writers, beyond their nationality or gender are, over and above everything, writers in their own right. Two years later, in her polemical lecture "The Asian Conspiracy" she went as far as to wonder: "Should one exit from the diasporic narrative to break this bind? Why not shift the gate?" (2010, 10). After having celebrated Filipino community in a most unconventional tale of food, family and longing (*Banana Heart Summer*, 2005), and having denounced Filipino poverty and the political shenanigans resulting from the global war on terror (*The Solemn Lantern Maker*, 2009), with the publication of *Fish-Hair Woman* (2012), her third novel, Bobis manages to shift the gate and, in this way, also shift perspectives. By introducing two white Australian characters in the remote and dangerous war zones in the Philippines, this Filipino Australian author locates Australia in Asia (rather than Asia in Australia), thus breaking away from the common migrant theme as expected in diaspora novels. Based on a previous short story with the same title in her celebrated collection *White Turtle* (1999), *Fish-Hair Woman* relies on magical realist strategies and defies conventional narrative modes in order to retrieve the painful memories of a traumatic past, and testify to the unutterable, to all that resists

*The research carried out for the writing of this article is part of a research project financed by the Spanish Ministry of Economy and Competitiveness (MINECO; code FFI2012-32719), and by the Government of Aragón and the European Social Fund (ESF; code H05).

straightforward representation, namely, the massacres and brutal destruction of whole villages, and the tragic disappearance of thousands of innocent and helpless people as a result of the militarization of the Philippines in the 1987–89 "Total War" waged by the dictatorial regime of President Ferdinand Marcos against communist insurgency.

The novel took 17 years to write and was rejected by six publishers – the "gatekeepers" of the Australian publishing industry, as Bobis calls them in "The Asian Conspiracy". *Fish-Hair Woman* was finally published by Spinifex in 2011. As Paul Giffard-Foret (2012) argues, one of the novel's main problems is its setting in a militarized village in the Philippines, meaning, therefore, that Australia and the Australian story are not central but rather remain in the background (para. 6). The dominant paradigm for the Asian Australian writer, Giffard-Foret continues, has so far been the "migrant story"; that is, a movement from Asia to Australia, and sometimes back to Asia so as to make it clear that the "Asian story" is Australian enough, but not quite. In this way, the Australian "gate" is safeguarded while "enriched" at the same time (para. 7). In clear contrast to this, Bobis's novel defiantly strives to reverse this movement in order to regionalize and dilute Australian identities by immersing white Australian characters in foreign and dangerous Asian settings instead. To quote Giffard-Foret's words again, "the hyphen in Asian Australian is not a straightforward road that can be easily co-opted into the migrant narrative, but a conflictive zone of incommensurability and 'abject' resistance writing back to the gatekeepers of the industry" (para. 8). As is well known, Australia's relationship with Asia has always been anything but easy. As David Walker (2013, 34), the knowledgeable Australian cultural historian, has argued, by the end of the 19th century Australia had established a number of relationships with the region to its north. Australia was certainly anxious at being taken over by populous Asia but, paradoxically, there was also a belief that, as an advanced democracy, Australia could and should set about playing a leading role in the region. As a result of the growth of Asia's political influence after the Second World War, more and more Australians started to believe that the future security and prosperity of their country would depend on how well they knew and understood Asia (as a matter of fact, Australia has always been concerned about its nearest neighbour, Indonesia, and of late China). Consequently, the sense of urgency over Asian engagement became stronger, mainly due to the growing economic power of some of their Asian neighbours. By the late 20th century it became clear for many political leaders and intellectuals that Australia needed to be accepted as part of Asia. While many Australians saw the ever-increasing power of some of their Asian neighbours (especially China) as a threat to the political stability of the region, they also took it that Australia, with its privileged status as a free-standing continent, was to look for and consolidate a leading role in regional affairs. The way in which Australia has been viewed and received in the region is of the utmost importance. Labour Prime Minister Kevin Rudd's dream to create a new Asia-Pacific community encountered many obstacles, above all because, all these good intentions notwithstanding, the fact remains that Australia has no deep affinity for the region and, even worse, some of its liberal policies still show racist hostilities to non-Europeans. Seeing Australia as outside Asia is by no means a thing of the past. Furthermore, the parochialism cultivated by a narrow conception of nationalism often creates a binary between the various groups living within a national border; this still shows in the way in which authors who, like Merlinda Bobis, have been living in Australia for years but were born in some of Australia's neighbouring Asian countries are seen and judged by many Australian publishing houses.

Like many other trauma narratives written in the wake of the Holocaust, *Fish-Hair Woman* discloses the contemporary "disquiet about memory [that] crystallized around the perception of two principal disorders: too *little memory*, and *too much*" (Terdiman 1993, 14; emphasis in original). Whereas both the Filipino government and the insurgency did their best to erase all traces of these atrocities in order to relegate them to oblivion, the victims were overwhelmed by the persistence of their traumatic past, to the point that they came to seem dominated, indeed possessed by it. Memory can be a burden, a crushing and painful activity and "is as susceptible as any other human faculty to abuse" (Rothberg 2009, 19). However, memory is also a responsibility, "a spur to unexpected acts of empathy and solidarity" (19), the mental activity that "connects us both to others and to reality itself" (Whitehead 2009, 87). Not only does *Fish-Hair Woman* testify to the need to remember but, very much in tune with the literary trend that came to be labelled as "historiographic metafiction", it also draws attention to its fictional nature and deliberately addresses the implied reader, as when Estrella, the Fish-Hair Woman, exclaims: "I will not allow you to invent me, you who read this, so I will tell you everything. Listen" (Bobis 2011, 4). Moreover, in keeping with other well-known historiographic metafictional novels, *Fish-Hair Woman* chooses to air marginalized voices and to "privilege the underclass – peasants, labourers, and the like – as agents of historical change" (Reyes 2008, 241) in what could be seen as an attempt to question official historical discourses (History vs. his/herstory). As Giffard-Foret (2012) claims, this is "a decolonizing gesture akin to the work of other Filipino scholars known as *Pantayong Pananaw* ('for-us-from-us' perspective)" (para. 6). It is clear that this novel focuses on the mysterious disappearance of Australian writer Tony McIntyre in the Philippines and on his son Luke's quest to find him there 13 years later. It contains all the ingredients of the oriental thriller: a revolution, a corrupt leader and a love affair with one of the "natives". However, it is also undeniable that *Fish-Hair Woman* refuses to offer yet another version of "the fictional Asia [westerners] used to know and love (or not know and fear)" (Broinowski 1999, para. 2).

Estrella, the novel's main character, is also the writer of the autobiographical magical realist manuscript that is embedded in, and interwoven with, the main and rather more realist narrative offered by an omniscient heterodiegetic narrator. This manuscript (chapters entitled "Beloved" and "Iraya" in the novel), tells the mythical story of the Fish-Hair Woman, also called Estrella, who was given this enigmatic name because she uses her hair to fish out corpses, victims of war, from the river. Just as the river transforms and changes its hue and scent (from lemon grass to brine) each time a body is thrown into the water, when-ever Estrella remembers something that makes her suffer, mainly her mournful mission to bring the dead back to the surface of the river, her hair inexorably grows.[1] "Hair. How was it linked with the heart? I'll tell you – it had something to do with memory. Every time I remembered anything that unsettled my heart, my hair grew one handspan" (Bobis 2011, 3).

Merlinda Bobis, born in the triply colonized Philippines – by Spain for nearly 400 years (1521–1898), America for 40 years (1901–45), then Japan for nearly five years (1941–45) – and now living in Australia, interlaces several localities/nationalities and their respec-tive languages and cultures in an artistic global imagined space. Similarly, her protagonist Estrella, a most important member of her community, but also alienated from it due to her subversive monstrosity, must constantly inhabit the liminal space that allows her to mediate between opposed realms: the familiar and unfamiliar, reality and magic, love and hate, life and death, earth and water, sanity and trauma, the villagers and the military, the Philippines and Australia, Bikol and English. Her body, and more particularly her hair, is the site of variegated tensions and contradictory meanings; notably, her hair stands for both her people's ultimate encapsulation of death and only desperate hope. These conflicting interpretations "unsettle the hybridity discourse normative to postcolonial analysis with trenchantly situated readings that stress enduring asymmetries of domination, injustice, racism, class dynamics, and uneven spatial development" (Wilson and Dissanayake [1996] 2005, 8). Consequently, unlike in many patriarchal/colonial signifying practices in which, Barbara Creed (1993) argues, the womb, and by extension the whole female body, is represented as a tomb, and thus as the ultimate embodiment of death and abjection, Estrella's hair, like its transnational author, transcends that demeaning homogenizing model in order to teem with threads which grow in ever multiple directions, thus criss-crossing unequal and discrepant allegiances and inheritances to bring forth what Homi Bhabha (1994) calls an "interstitial" or "third space" born of the imaginative negotiation of "incommensurable differences" (217–218). With her ever-growing hair hurting with history, Estrella remains, to quote Hamid Naficy's term, in "agonistic liminality" ([1996] 2005, 124); that is, halfway between devastation and redemption, abjection and subversion. Estrella's impossible condition wonderfully encapsulates the author's "position as subject inhabiting transnational and exilic spaces, where [she] travel[s] in the slip-zone of fusion and admixture" (124), the one and only zone which can allow for dialectical vision, for the integration of sameness and difference, continuity and discontinuity, in a globalized world ever so complex and changing.

For Bobis, literature starts with the body. As she once stated (Rutledge 2010; para. 5–6), stories find her, first through the ear, and from there, to the heart, where they grow and expand. In the 1990s, when she could not find a publisher for her poems, she decided to perform them, to "buil[d her] niche, not by changing [her] voice but by performing it – bringing to [her] audience *the body with the text*. A body-to-body encounter" (Bobis 2008; para. 19; emphasis in original). Bobis discovered the body as the perfect medium for storytelling. "The body telling a story is visceral and also ephemeral, but paradoxically unforgettable at its best" (as quoted in Rutledge 2010; para. 6), she affirms. Not in vain does *Fish-Hair Woman* contain so many references to body parts and secretions: breath, sweat, skin, anus, throat, navel, chest, groin, gut, heart, mouth, tongue and, above all, hair, Estrella's magical long hair that grows each time she senses violence and pain, strands of hair that "would not stop growing into story after story, into all that [she] can remember […]. Stories that can save, that can kill" (Bobis 2011, 137). As Giffard-Foret (2012) has put it, "through the bodily metaphor of hair-growing, weaving and unknotting, remembering and forgetting, the reader is caught into the rhizomic nets of 'text-ility' " (para. 15). Stories flow into each other, become one continuous low humming sound that brings back memories of the beloved, thus soothing trauma, bringing endless past and present versions together, and corroborating Michael Rothberg's contention that memory is "multidirectional", since it […] cuts across and binds together diverse spatial, temporal, and cultural sites" (2009, 11). It is up to readers, then, to listen to them all in order to establish all pertinent connections across time and space, fill in the gaps, look for meaning, and eventually make them their own:

> So dear reader, when your eyes pass over these stories, consider your capacity to gather all of them, even the gaps in between, those that I dare not tell or do not know of yet or perhaps would never even imagine, but which might be utterly clear to you. Why my memories weave in and out of death and love. [… B]ecause each encounter threads a million others. The capillaries of love and war flow into each other, into a handspan of hair. (Bobis 2011, 142)

Moreover, in keeping with Proust's (1913–27) ideas as put forward in his seminal novel *À la recherche du temps tempu*, Bobis's works corroborate the belief that the body is also essential to the memory that grasps the past in its entirety, reviving not only memory images, but also related sensations and emotions (what Proust labels as "involuntary memory"). The body, and in particular the senses, play a crucial role in resurrecting the past, since they act as a repository of remembered locations and recollections of all kinds (Whitehead 2009, 104–105). "Can anyone miss the stories of the body?" Bobis (2011), Estrella wonders (Bobis 2011, 10). If the sense of sight is undoubtedly important, Bobis's works, like Proust's, often depict it as an unreliable guardian of the past, and privilege instead the physical senses of taste and smell. The eyes can fail us; that is why the fireflies are so necessary: they light the dead so that they can be found. However, as the novel seems to suggest, while the eyes can easily lie to us, the other senses provide us with rather more reliable memories. Accordingly, recurring images, sounds and smells permeate the whole text. As Pay Inyo, the kind-hearted gravedigger, affirms, "to keep a place alive in your heart, it must dwell in your mouth" (201); naming preserves memories and brings the dead back to life. One of the novel's recurrent smells is the sweetness of the lemongrass that "aspires to flavour all of the earth" (289), and desperately strives to smother brine, the saltiness of the corpses dumped into the river. However, the smell of death cannot be easily removed either, "as if death were offended that anyone should deny it" (181). Similarly, there are sounds that bring individuals back to their past traumatic scenarios: Luke, like the deadly wind, howls in his dreams and whenever he is confronted with death, just as he was the day he found the dead body of his mother after she committed suicide; and Adora, the Filipino girl whom he will eventually marry, is possessed by the sound of the jeep's tyres that she heard the night she and her little brother got shot.

Fish-Hair Woman contains a multitude of stories that demand to be unwoven, voiced, deciphered. On the one hand, stories of poor farmers' unfair expropriation by powerful and merciless *mestizos* and their ruthless private army, the *Anghel de la Guardia*; stories of rape, torture, and murder by the State with the cynical complicity of the west, including Australia. On the other hand, stories of well-meaning Australian activists who, like Tony, mainly want to make up for their past mistakes and "pardon" (42) themselves by reporting on these Third World massacres yet hope that this is merely a short stint, since they will soon leave this beautiful but turbulent country to go back to their safe and comfortable homes. Like other well-known magical-realist novels, such as those written by García Marquez, *Fish-Hair Woman* is a family saga full of compelling characters, each of whom has his/her own heartbreaking story to tell and unravel. At once a love story, a war story, a family story, a murder mystery, a political thriller, "a fairy tale, a melodrama, and a myth" (293), Bobis's novel spans three different decades and continents, from the Marcos regime's "Total War" against the New People's Army (NPA), the military branch of the Communist Party, to the February 1986 People Power Revolution and into the year 1997. At this point Luke travels to the Philippines from Sydney after having received a mysterious and cryptic note, allegedly sent by his dying father after 13 years of silence, but when he arrives at Manila airport his father is nowhere to be seen. The man who is awaiting him instead is Dr Alvarado, who claims to be a close friend of his father's and has just returned from years of political exile in Hawaii. The main characters are Estrella, Pilar, her older "sister" who will soon become part of the communist insurgency, and Tony, the Australian journalist. The three of them make up a curious love triangle, as the two women will respectively fall in love with the same Australian man. To make matters even more complicated, Estrella, whose birth brought about her mother's death, happens to be the illegitimate daughter of Dr Alvarado (Mayor and then Governor Kiko Estradero). When Estrella's grandmother dies of grief soon after her daughter dies, it is Mamay Dulce, the village midwife and mother of Pilar and Bolodoy, who pledges to take care of Estrella as if she were her own daughter. While the main action takes place in 1987, the novel narrates events that occurred over three decades (in 1977, 1987 and 1997), and most of the story is being told from the perspective of 1997. By this time, Pilar and Tony are among the dead or *desaparecidos*, and Tony's son, Luke, has been invited to visit the Philippines by Dr Alvarado, who makes Luke believe that his father is still alive so that he can use the son to conceal his shameful past and facilitate his return to politics. Past and present can in no way become disentangled. The constant merging of memory with the present often gives the prose the quality of a dream, or rather of the nightmare of a never-ending battle for, no matter how hard we try, "the present cannot be knotted in place with the past, because they're jealous of each other, they fight for prominence in the heart" (258). Belated traumas must be acted out again and again, in a desperate attempt to be worked through, but old-time traumatic experiences cannot always be acknowledged and overcome, and past and present thus remain the two irreconcilable sides of the same traumatic coin.

Similarly, the magical-realist story of Estrella, the Fish-Hair Woman, who can be said to speak for those living on the margins, and the realistic account of the life of Stella which, being the story of Dr Alvarado's biological daughter, might somehow be regarded as partly appropriated and controlled by those holding power, can be seen as complementary versions of the same traumatic history. For the sake of clarity, it must be stated that Stella is the name that Estrella is given when she is taken to Hawaii by her father after the tragic deaths of Pilar and Bolodoy. The use of both names, apparently different but also identical, is by no means accidental, since it clearly contributes to generating confusion and blurring the boundaries between the magical-realist manuscript and the realist story within which it is embedded. Are Estrella and Stella one and the same woman, or is Estrella Stella's ghostly projection? The novel offers no clear answer to this question. In keeping with many Filipino traditional stories, myth and reality are conflated, and it is up to readers to keep them together or drive them apart. This ambiguity notwithstanding, in the writing of this article I have tried to be faithful to the name the novel uses in its different sections. As is always the case with palimpsests, the two stories (Estrella's and Stella's) contain and mirror each other (the same and the other conflate), and therefore disclose the multilayered nature of reality, and by extension history, which, as Foucault ([1977], 1996) argues in "Nietzsche, Genealogy, History", is nothing but a collection of palimpsestuous documents. The neologism "palimpsestuous" clearly points to the complex textual relationality embodied in the palimpsest. Although, as Sarah Dillon (2006) explains, the process that generates palimpsests is one of layering, the result of this process is a surface structure that can be best described by the term "involuted", which De Quincey coined in his 1845 seminal essay "The Palimpsest", a resurrective fantasy with which he attempted to secure the continued life of his dead sister Elizabeth (Dillon 2006, 244). Accordingly, the palimpsest is, to quote Dillon, "an involuted phenomenon where otherwise unrelated texts are involved and entangled, intricately interwoven, interrupting and inhabiting each other" (245). Thus, "where 'palimpsestic' refers to the process of layering that produces a palimpsest, 'palimpsestuous' describes the structure with which one is presented as a result of that process, and the subsequent reappearance of the underlying script" (245). To put it differently, the present of the palimpsest implies the presence of texts from the past, while it remains open to further inscription by texts of the future, and the presence of all these texts does not do away with temporality, but rather testifies to the spectrality of any present moment, which will always encapsulate and subsume past, present and future moments. Moreover, as Dillon concludes, the structure of the palimpsest also embodies the relationship of cryptic haunting on which Derrida elaborates in *Specters of Marx* (1994), whereby the past and the dead can live on (Dillon 2006, 249). Taking all this into account, it might be argued that Estrella and Stella's stories are the two main encrypted texts that make up the palimpsest fabric of Bobis's novel. Readers are consequently compelled to undertake a palimpsestuous reading, the ultimate aim of which is not so much to discover the roots of individual and cultural identity, but rather to prioritize their dissipation, and by extension to draw readers' attention to the various systems of subjection that constitute history as a violent and repeated palimpsestuous play of dominations and forces. In short, the palimpsest fabric of Bobis's novel can be argued as playing a fundamental role to represent history, not as natural evolution or progress (as advocated by Enlightenment thought), but rather as the history of colonial expansion and conquest, consisting of not just the violent erasure and superimposition of cultures, but also the defiant and subversive resilience and persistence of the colonized.

It is no wonder that the Fish-Hair Woman's story should belong in the realm of magical realism. As critics such as Christopher Warnes (2014) have affirmed, magical realism represents the writing back of the margins to the centre, the questioning of the binaries of modern thought and the assumptions of the Enlightenment, and the disclosure of the limitations of European rationalism and of the ethical failings of realism (6). Furthermore, to turn to Lévy-Bruhl's (1926) terminology, magical realism may be said to represent an attempt to supplement, extend or overwhelm the law of causality (the logical mentality) with the law of participation (the mystic mentality). Lévy-Bruhl spoke of the existence of a mystic mentality, quite different from modern causal logic. For this critic, mystic "implies a belief in forces and influences and actions which, though imperceptible to sense, are nevertheless real" (38). This belief inexorably means that there is no difference between natural and supernatural: "The primitive's mentality does not recognize two distinct worlds in contact with one another and more or less penetrating. To him there is but one" (68). This type of thought was ruled by what he labelled as the law of participation, the main characteristic of which is spatial and temporal fusion. On the contrary, the logical mentality is ruled by the law of causality which, being conceptual, empirical and scientifically rational, strives to identify and do away with all sorts of contradictions. One of the main reasons why writers like Bobis resort to magical realism is, therefore, their need to reveal the causal paradigm as flawed, mainly because it was the outcome of the emergence and development of modernity and the colonial expansion that it propitiated. As Warnes (2014) puts it:

> For these postcolonial writers, [magical realism] is tainted by its association with colonialism and neo-colonialism. As a postcolonial response to colonialism's often brutal enforcing of a selectively-conceived modernity, magical realism of this kind seeks to reclaim what has been lost: knowledge, values, traditions, ways of seeing, beliefs. In this model, the horizons of the causal paradigm are extended to include events and possibilities that would ordinarily be circumscribed. (12)

The palimpsestic nature of Bobis's novel, in which different stories, modes of writing, and temporal and spatial coordinates are not separate from one another but entwined and encoded in one another, testifies to the fact that colonized and colonizing discourses are interwoven, each affecting and inhabiting the other, which in turn embodies their potential to prompt future re-inscriptions and shifts in the balances of power.

The novel is divided into five chapters ("Beloved", "Gestures", "Iraya", "Testimonies" and "River"). Chapters 1 and 3, written in the first and third person, are Estrella's manuscript about her life until the war breaks out. According to Sing (2011, para. 6), "the manuscript is the magic of this magical realist novel", and the transitions between chapters often seem to be a sudden move back to, or beyond, reality; from the lyrical and enhancing storytelling of Estrella to the rather more straightforward prose narrating the stories of the Australians and Estrella's relatives and neighbours in Iraya. Bobis also clings to her bilingual tradition of including Filipino words and expressions in the text, which can have the double and contradictory effect of engaging while also disturbing many readers. To make the narrative even more complicated, the rest of the story is told by an unnamed narrator, who examines the handling of the events of the manuscript in the present by Stella, Luke and many other characters, who offer their own stories through changing and multiple points of view, making connections, like those between past and present, that can often be tumultuous and difficult to identify on a first reading. *Fish-Hair Woman* is, to quote Tristan Foster's words, "a narrative of knots" (2012, para. 1), a novel as complex as the world. That is why stories and myths are so necessary; they can help us to cope with this chaos, since they are a wonderful "attempt at ordering a universe that stubbornly refuses to offer up a reason" (para. 3). Last but not least, the story is told through six newspaper clippings in the *Philippine Daily News*, which open and close the novel, and appear in between the five different parts into which the novel is divided. While the stories told by the different characters are compelling and saturated with heartbreaking traumatic events and silences, the clippings only expose how disturbingly detached and devoid of meaning media reports can be, how little of reality they contain, and how many atrocities and traumas they conceal. The novel's structure wonderfully mimics the way we layer stories, intertwine history and myth, reality and fantasy, stories and memories, including public and official discourses and those forbidden and hidden under lock and key. This hyperabundance of stories can baffle many readers, who may find it difficult to understand and assemble them into a coherent whole. Even the gravedigger Pay Inyo, one of the most humane characters in the story, in charge of helping the dead cross to the other side and recipient of most of the characters' secrets, does not know what to do with the story:

> But who is the hero in this story? Pay Inyo is not sure anymore, nor is he sure about what the story is in the first place. There are too many stories weaving into each other, only to unweave themselves at each telling, so that each story can claim prominence. Stories are such jealous things. The past and the present, ay, what wayward strands. (Bobis 2011, 259)

Fish-Hair Woman is, above all, a harrowing read, a story about collective grieving and collective responsibility, a novel which claims, to quote Gail Jones's words on the cover of the novel, "that testimony is solidarity and that the loss and retrieval of any story of historical suffering implicates us all". Estrella feels the compulsive need to retrieve corpses and tell the victims' stories so that they can come to the surface and are never forgotten, thus enabling some kind of retributive justice finally to be done. Following LaCapra's (2001) ideas, it could be argued that Estrella's act of retrieval is an example of "empathic unsettlement", this being understood as "a kind of virtual experience through which one puts oneself in the other's position while recognizing the difference of that position and hence not taking the other's place" (78). It might also be concluded that Estrella wants to make her readers aware that trauma is not only the silent psychic response of an individual to an overwhelmingly pain-ful or terrifying event, but is also a symbol of horror in a society that is possessed by the angst of having finally understood the atrocities that apparently normal human beings are capable of perpetrating (Granofsky 1995, 2). However, another less positive interpretation could also be given. If we cling to the idea put forward by trauma scholars such as Kalí Tal (1996) that survivor accounts are the only acceptable form of trauma testimony, then it follows that Estrella's manuscript can be criticized as a wrongful appropriation of other people's traumas that attempts to fit the trauma experience into a literary convention that will allow her own narrative voice to be invented. Furthermore, as Professor Inez Carillo, Estrella's old-time classmate, contends, it could also be added that Estrella is not bearing witness to the victims' suffering, but is rather co-opting, appropriating their memories and Iraya's myth in order to be vindicated. According to Inez, Estrella Estradero Alvarado

> turned against her family, her country, her heart […]. She left us all in the seventies, then wrote herself clean in this manuscript. She has written herself in the place of her sister, and in the place of a myth – you know […] Iraya did believe in a Fish-Hair Woman. Despair makes you believe in anything. It fuels fervour, it is its own religion. (Bobis 2011, 228–229)

Trauma and shame conflate in Stella's persona. As is well known, trauma has often been described as the response to an overwhelming violent event or events which can only be acknowledged at belated stages, when the trauma seems to repeat itself in forms of post-traumatic symptoms such as nightmares or flashbacks (Caruth 1996, 91–92). Following Freud's ideas, Estrella's dream of angels descending upside down and of coffins hanging from trees (Bobis 2011, 140), but above all her fantastic hair, could be regarded as hysterical symptoms that are closely linked to her buried traumatic childhood mem-ories: that of her birth, which claimed her mother's life and deprived Estrella of any hair, and that of her lethal fall off the fart-fart tree, when Pilar made her fly as if she were the Easter angel. Such was the traumatic shock she suffered that it was only after she recov-ered from this fall that her hair finally began to grow, and then did so out of measure. Pay Inyo declared her head "capable of wonderful things, then suggested that [she] probably had some secret powers inside. Thus the mythmaking began" (139): a mythmaking that would determine her future relationships with the people from Iraya. Furthermore, when in 1987 Tony visited Dr Alvarado in Hawaii to ask for his help in finding Pilar, he told Stella many sad and scary stories. After Tony left, Adora remembers, Stella internalized all that pain and suffered post-traumatic stress disorder. On the other hand, Stella is also ashamed that her father should be responsible for all those deaths, and that she had left all her loved ones behind. That is why she takes her final revenge on her father; she kills him and takes his corpse back to Iraya, where she makes sure that he is shamed in his own house and is finally buried in a public cemetery with no priest. Moreover, Stella knows that the village, in loathing him, also loathes her mother and herself. In other words, she is punishing her father, but also herself, and she does this out of shame. Shame has often been defined as a painful, burdensome and self-reflexive feeling whereby the subject's sense of herself, her role and relationship with her world are shattered. The self feels that she has failed to meet her personal and social expectations. As a consequence, she internalizes the negative, self-diminishing and destructive feelings generally associated with defeat, and feels humiliated and exposed. In Stella's case, trauma and shame go hand in hand. Trauma shatters her trust in the solidity of her social bonds and her own self. Her fear of being left alone is accentuated; hence her desperate attempt to bring all her loved ones back with her stories. Furthermore, since stigma is attached to her ever-growing hair, her most outstanding post-traumatic symptom, she falls into a spiral of shame and acting out. The more she exposes her grief, the more aware she becomes of the negative feelings attached to it, and thus the more she resists facing them. Her search for empathic and supportive readers therefore becomes imperative. She must keep on weaving one story into another, in a desperate attempt to narrativize all these traumatic memories and be listened to, but the pain she must face up to is simply unbearable. She may not be able to find any answers, but must keep on looking for them. The novel's epigraph on its preliminary unnumbered pages speaks for itself:

> Why do these things happen?
>
> I cannot find an answer.
>
> I can only try to lay the question in its place.

Language can be deemed totally futile when confronted with grief, pain and irretrievable losses: "This is a silence no one can ever write and least of all rewrite", Estrella affirms (Bobis, 2011, 58). And yet more and more stories must be told so that this difficult ethical encounter with the other can be possible, so that we can all cross to the other side and become aware of our common human condition.

> This is the wake of the world: each of us standing around a pool that we have collected for centuries. We are looking in with our little pails. […] We try to find only what is ours. We wring our hands. Ay, how to go home with only my undiluted pail of grief? To wash my rice with or my babies, to drink? But the water is my dead kin, an enemy, a beloved, a stranger, a friend, someone who loved me or broke my heart. How to tell them apart? How to cleave water from water? (276)

Opening oneself up to the trauma of another can lead to cross-cultural understanding and to the possibility of new forms of community. It is only when we become aware of this potential that we can face difficult times with resilience and live in hope. It must be noted, however, that hope should never be confused with optimism. As Wendy O'Brien (2010) argues, hope "is not the conviction that something will turn out well, but the certainty that something makes sense, regardless of how it turns out" (30). Hope makes us human, makes us free; hope reminds us of what the human condition is all about, of its privileges and its responsibilities. Following Stella's command, Luke finishes her story with his and tells the world (Bobis 2011, 287). However, the ending Luke provides is of a rather more positive nature. If Stella's story could only finish with her own death, Luke's story is one of love, life and hope, wonderfully embodied in the figure of his little daughter, Adora-Estrella. "Love is our main cause after all" (179), Estrella wrote. Luke has finally understood what Pan Inyo knew only too well, and becomes fully aware of when he contemplates his daughter, all enveloped in the light of dozens of fireflies: that this collective pool of grief can also be, is, our collective pool of joy (303).

Fish-Hair Woman is much more than an Asian Australian story, since it is also part of the big global picture. It is the unlimited multiplicity at work within the text, or, rather, the text's ultimate palimpsestuous liminality, that turns this transnational novel into a source of never-ending scenarios and possibilities, into an ultimately ethical project, which consequently manages to put the question of justice in its place by exceeding the limits of former reductive postcolonial interpretations. It is Estrella's capacity to open herself up to absolute otherness that allows her to represent what ultimately transcends the limits of representation, to contract space and time, to become the catalyst that alone can contest and lump together distinct but entangled worlds and cosmovisions. Similarly, her ever-growing hair becomes a tool of reconciliation and resistance that brings to the fore the problems involved in trying to live with multiple identities and the demand for justice. Not in vain does her name – Estrella/Stella – encapsulate apparently contradictory meanings: on the one hand, "star", "light" (hope); on the other hand, "trace", "shadow" (trauma's perennial marks on people's psyche and the survivors' subsequent compulsory demand for justice). Estrella's monstrous hair "express[es] and encode[s] the melo(drama) of transnational subjectivity", since it inexorably blurs and negotiates "the boundaries between self and other, female and male, inside and outside, homeland and hostland" (Naficy [1996] 2005, 128–129). Bearing all this in mind, it can be concluded that Bobis's novel manages to open up space for an ongoing transformative dialogue across barriers of language, nationality, gender, race and class, which can somehow contribute not only to questioning any official articulations of a sense of identity (Australian in this case) inspired by a unitarian nationalist model, but also to making amends for the traumatic past resulting from colonial violence and paving the way for hope in a better future.

Note

1. Estrella and her prodigious hair inevitably bring to mind the figure of Medusa, the Greek mythological guardian. However, whereas Medusa's monstrosity is endowed with an utterly negative nature, Estrella's fate consists in using her hair to allow the living to retrieve, mourn and pay their due respect to the dead. In an attempt to look for connections with contemporary literary texts, interesting similarities can be found between Bobis's Estrella and the Salt Fish Girl, the eponymous heroine of Canadian professor Larissa Lai's 2002 novel, which also encompasses stories of many varieties, including fantastical fiction and magical realism.

Disclosure statement

No potential conflict of interest was reported by the author.

References

Bhabha, Homi. 1994. *The Location of Culture*. London and New York: Routledge.
Bobis, Merlinda. 2008. "Voice-Niche-Brand: Marketing Asian-Australianness." *Australian Humanities Review* 45. http://www.australianhumanitiesreview.org/archive/Issue-November-2008/bobis.html
Bobis, Merlinda. 2010. "The Asian Conspiracy: Deploying Voice/Deploying Story." *Australian Literary Studies* 25 (3): 1–19.

Bobis, Merlinda. 2011. *Fish-Hair Woman*. Melbourne: Spinifex.

Broinowski, Alison. 1999. "The No-Name Australians and the Missing Subaltern. Asian Australian Fiction." Paper presented at the Asian Australian Identities Conference, ANU (Australian National University), Canberra, September 27–29. https://digitalcollections.anu.edu.au/bitstream/1885/41894/1/asia_fiction.html

Caruth, Cathy. 1996. *Unclaimed Experience: Trauma, Narrative and History*. Baltimore MD: Johns Hopkins University Press.

Creed, Barbara. 1993. *The Monstrous Feminine: Film, Feminism, Psychoanalysis*. London and New York: Routledge.

Derrida, Jacques. 1994. *Specters of Marx: The State of the Debt, the Work of Mourning, and the New International*. Translated by Peggy Kamuf. New York and London: Routledge.

Dillon, Sarah. 2006. "Reinscribing De Quincey's Palimpsest: The Significance of the Palimpsest in Contemporary Literary and Cultural Studies." *Textual Practice* 19 (3): 243–263.

Foster, Tristan. 2012. "Untruths Sculpted into Truths: Merlinda Bobis's *Fish-Hair Woman*." *Verity La*. http://verityla.com/untruths-sculpted-into-truths-tristan-foster

Foucault, Michael. [1977] 1996. "Nietzsche, Genealogy, History." In *Language, Counter-Memory, Practice: Selected Essays and Interviews*. Translated by Donald F. Bouchard, and Sherry Simon, and edited with an introduction by Donald F. Bouchard, 139–164. Ithaca, NY: Cornell University Press.

Giffard-Foret, Paul. 2012. "Silencing Voice, Voicing Silence: A Review of *Fish-Hair Woman*." *Mascara: Literary Review*. http://mascarareview.com/paul-giffard-foret-reviews-fish-hair-woman-by-merlinda-bobis

Granofsky, Ronald. 1995. *The Trauma Novel: Contemporary Symbolic Depictions of Collective Disaster*. New York: Peter Lang.

LaCapra, Dominick. 2001. *Writing History, Writing Trauma*. Baltimore MD: Johns Hopkins University Press.

Lévy-Bruhl, Lucien. 1926. *How Natives Think*. London: George Allen Unwin.

Naficy, Hamid. [1996] 2005. "Phobic Spaces and Liminal Panics: Independent Transnational Film Genre." In *Global/Local. Cultural Production and the Transnational Imaginary*, edited by Rob Wilson, and Wimal Dissanayake, 119–144. Durham and London: Duke University Press.

O'Brien, Wendy. 2010. "Exercise of Hope." In *The Resilience of Hope*, edited by Janette McDonald, and Andrea M. Stephenson, 29–39. Amsterdam and New York: Rodopi.

Proust, Marcel. [1913–27] 1922–31. In *Search of Lost Time*. Translated by C.K. Scott-Moncrieff, Stephen Hudson, Terence Kilmartin, Lydia Davis, and James Grieve. Paris: Grasset and Gallimard.

Reyes, Portia L. 2008. "Fighting over a Nation: Theorizing a Filipino Historiography." *Postcolonial Studies* 11 (3): 241–258.

Rothberg, Michael. 2009. *Multidirectional Memory: Remembering the Holocaust in the Age of Decolonization*. Stanford CA: Stanford University Press.

Rutledge, Renee Macalino. 2010. "Painting with Words, Writing with the Body: Genre-Hopping with Merlinda Bobis." *Filipinas on-Line: The Community Journal for Filipinos Worldwide*. http://www.filipinasmag.com/?p=85

Sing, Teagan Kum. 2011. "Crossing the Boundary: Raising the Issues We Prefer to Ignore." *Fishing for Stories-University of Queensland*. http://www.emsah.uq.edu.au/awsr/new_site/awbr_archive/151/bobis.html

Tal, Kalí. 1996. *Worlds of Hurt: Reading the Literatures of Trauma*. Cambridge: Cambridge University Press.

Terdiman, Richard. 1993. *Present past: Modernity and the Memory Crisis*. London and New York: Cornell University Press.

Walker, David. 2013. *Experiencing Turbulence: Asia in the Australian Imaginary*. New Delhi: Readworthy.

Warnes, Christopher. 2014. *Magical Realism and the Postcolonial Novel: Between Faith and Irreverence*. London: Palgrave MacMillan.

Whitehead, Anne. 2009. *Memory*. London and New York: Routledge.

Wilson, Rob, and Wimal Dissanayake. [1996] 2005. "Introduction: Tracking the Global/Local." In *Global/Local. Cultural Production and the Transnational Imaginary*, edited by Rob Wilson, and Wimal Dissanayake, 1–18. Durham and London: Duke University Press.

Re-storying the past, re-imagining the future in Adib Khan's *Homecoming* and *Spiral Road*

Stefano Mercanti

ABSTRACT

This article argues that Adib Khan's fiction challenges the orthodoxies of rigid cultural boundaries and dominator systems by creatively reconfiguring histories, landscapes and identities into forms of transcultural dialogue. Both *Homecoming* (2003) and *Spiral Road* (2007) tell the story of the disquieted lives of their protagonists, Martin and Masud, who struggle to inhabit an empathetic consciousness in a world ranked and measured by labels, points of origin, skin colour and religion. Their sense of displacement and yearning to belong – a feature in all Khan's novels – enable them to move beyond the anxieties of finding a fitting place within the culture around them and embrace new ways of overcoming disconnection, violence and other forms of cultural stereotyping common to all cultures, thus rethinking their past and recreating a more equitable future.

Multi-award-winning novelist, Adib Khan (b. 1949), who migrated from Bangladesh to Australia in 1973, holds a significant place on the Australian literary scene.[1]

Yet, for all the critical attention his work has gained along with that of other prominent diasporic authors, Asian Australian cultural production has remained relegated to the periphery of the Australian literary canon. Despite the normative expectations and hierarchical ideals of Australian national literature – reluctant to expand its insular Anglo Celtic parameters – South Asian Australian writing has, since the 1950s when Meena Abdulla's fiction was first published,[2] been developing into an influential field of literary and critical production. Writing itself, as Khan commented 15 years ago, "is beginning to assume more importance than the obsession with an ossified literary identity that is presumably meant to define the core of Australian culture" (2000, 1) and today South Asian writing continually flourishes "as a part and parcel of the truly 'Australian made' experience" (Sarwal 2015, 122). After all, even if Kirkpatrick and Dixon's (2012) call in their *Republic of Letters* for Australian literature and literary studies to reach out to the world has resulted only in muted rearrangements of the furniture, "a new literary category is being written into being" (Ommundsen 2012, 5). With the advent of the ever-growing cultural production of Asian Australian writers, the landscape is undoubtedly changing, as Nicholas Jose (2015) also concurs. More importantly, Asian Australian writing has found a prominent place in the proposed Australian National English curriculum where students will "explore and appreciate the rich tradition of texts from and about the peoples and countries of Asia, including texts written by Asian Australians" (Australian Curriculum, Assessment and Reporting Authority [ACARA] 2011, 15). From this it can be inferred that stereotypical views of Asian and Australian spaces and identities are being reconfigured within the ongoing tensions between different cultures, both indigenous and adopted, offering "representational alternatives to the longstanding, projection of Australian-European identity" (Helff 2009, 142).

What is most fascinating about South Asian Australian writers, like other migrant writers elsewhere, is how distinctive they are in their exploration of certain themes and geographies of mind and being, intellectual as well as political, which do not neatly fit within national, cultural and linguistic borders, thus enabling readers to pull down artificial barriers and see both themselves and their homelands in a new light. Particularly pressing in Khan's novels is the exploration of the difficulties of belonging to different cultural traditions – his innate "place polygamy" (Khan 2013, 189), as he puts it – and of being outside "dominator models" to explicitly challenge traditions of violence, conflict and other forms of inequality and oppression. Here, I use the terms "dominator" and "partnership" as propounded by the eminent macro-historian and systems scientist Riane Eisler (1987) to identify two fundamental ways of structuring social relations: the "dominator model" based on social systems characterized by an authoritarian and inequitable family, social, political and economic structure of rigid hierarchies of oppression with a high degree of fear, abuse and violence; and the "partnership model" hinging on the principle of linking rather than ranking, and honouring cultural diversity and inclusion through mutually respectful relationships based on caring, equality and empathy. As Eisler observes:

> The partnership system and the domination system are self-organizing and nonlinear. They describe mutually supporting interactions of key systems components that maintain a particular systems configuration. These interactions establish and maintain two very different types of relations – from intimate to international. One type is based on rigid rankings of domination ultimately backed up by fear and force. The other type is based on mutual respect, mutual accountability, and mutual benefit. (Eisler 2014, 4)

As a growing field of interdisciplinary critical inquiry, partnership studies situates cross-cultural encounters within Eisler's partnership model in order to transcend the old dominator in-group-versus-out-group rankings in favour of a mutuality negotiated on the "linking" of human relationships. The aim is effectively to prevent the absorption of heterogeneous identities into the same old hegemonic dominator systems, which structurally rely on exclusivist sameness and homogeneity.[3] Within this theoretical framework, cultural differences are instead seen as "relational" and successfully celebrated in a real sense of shared humanity underpinning every multi-ethnic society, "to effectively move beyond neo-colonial systems, which often cast non-Western cultures as inferior partners confined within asymmetrical power relationships" (Riem 2015, 8). Attempts to challenge western hegemonies in a supposedly postcolonial, globalized world perpetrates similar unequal binary power relationships if oppositional strategies based on a "superior-inferior" model of culture (e.g. the west and its others) are adopted. To put it more simply, as one of Khan's protagonists comments, "Postcolonial? […] That word's a construct of English Departments and Centres of Cultural Studies in certain parts of the world. There is nothing *post* about colonialism. Merely a shift in modus operandi" (Khan 2007, 12; emphasis in original). Hence the need for different discursive practices that do not so much deconstruct dominator western ideologies as go beyond the binary power hierarchies they embody, and emphasize the ongoing dialogic interactions – "the partnership" – across different cultural traditions, and more extensively among human relationships, taking new steps toward the construction of a more equalitarian,[4] mutual vision of culture.

Eisler's partnership model provides a crucial frame for my reading of Khan's fiction, which aims to show how the main characters' quest for identity becomes the privileged playground in which their disquieted selves are constantly reconfigured and recreated by transcending "domination hierarchies".[5] The analysis will show that by merging into a partnership consciousness rooted in relational connections based on empathy, mutual trust and non-violence, their intellectual and emotional horizons are extended, their desire to explore new territories recharged and the richness of cultural diversity celebrated, enabling them to surmount rigid cultural parochialism, legacies of violence and conflict. Khan's nuanced investigation into the conditions that perpetrate structural violence and cultural division shows that these can be overcome by transcending the usual dominator demarcation of an "us" versus "them" and embracing diversity through mutually symmetrical and caring relationships; in this way he re-examines unproblematic notions of essential cultural differences and allows our highest human potential for empathy and compassion to be realized.

Khan's unwavering refusal to belong to a monocultural society has characterized his entire oeuvre since the publication of his first novel *Seasonal Adjustments* (1994), in which both South Asia and Australia are constantly seen in their multifaceted cross-cultural encounters. In this partly autobiographical novel, the protagonist, Iqbal, returns to Bangladesh to visit his family after 18 years, moved by "a keen desire to begin anew, a spirit of generosity toward oneself, a renewal of faith in humanity and a burning energy to create a new social order whose virtues are not merely remote ideals" (Khan 1994, 261). However, he sees his native country "with the critical eyes of an intolerant alien" (46) and is relieved that he does not live there any more. Equally disappointing is his view of Australia, which he sees as an immature youth tottering on the brink of adulthood, struggling to come to terms with ageing and self-responsibility, and this contributes to his feeling a stranger wherever he goes. This perception reinforces his deep conviction that "the most important identity is that of a human being" (250) and deepens his awareness of an ever-growing composite of diverse cultures. In a world where human relationships are predominantly measured by "the fallacy of cultural superiority" (33), he finds himself unable to identify with a single mainstream tradition or place, and these very tensions arising from his fragmented self enable him to posit both xenophobia and rigid religious orthodoxy under the spotlight as the oppressive dominator systems which he struggles to transcend.[6]

Khan readdresses the same themes of family, home and yearnings for love and connection as well as the memory of the past in *Solitude of Illusions* (1996), by focusing on an elderly character, Khalid, a prominent businessman afflicted by a terminal illness. He leaves his home in Calcutta to visit his Australian son, an encounter which provokes issues arising from generational conflicts and changing living conditions. As Khalid comes close to death, memories of his youth become his sole consolation: "the past rarely appeared as a coherent sequence. It came out of memory like a handful of confetti which drifted beyond Khalid Sharif before he could catch one and linger with its significance" (Khan 1996, 12–13). As a young man, he was sent to a house of courtesans for a sexual education and, against all conventions, he fell in love with Nazli: "she was meant to teach him about manners and behaviour, about love-making and its pleasures beyond the act itself. Instead, he learned about the vulnerability of the human heart and the way it defies reason" (102). Compelled to leave her by both their outraged families, he is burdened by this enforced separation with guilt and self-reproach, and haunted for the rest of his life. Often reflecting on the intricate mechanism of existence, Khalid emerges as a contemplative and anxious character struggling to be himself beyond the expectations of mainstream patriarchal family responsibilities and asserting the dignifying vulnerability of being simply human throughout the hazards of life's unexpected turns.

Khan's desire to see how far he can stretch his imagination and defiantly expose the fundamental dominator flaws of conventional society takes shape in Vamana, the protagonist of *The Storyteller* (2000), a misshapen and ugly bisexual storytelling dwarf living in the slums of New Delhi. His stories are fuelled by words that deflate hierarchies, stereotypes and normative models of writing about people, countries or communities of origin: "a metaphor, a reminder of our creative natures and an indictment on how we have crippled and distorted ourselves, failing our potential as human beings" (Greet 2000, 11). Abandoned by his parents, Vamana is adopted by a woman who sees beyond the child's deformity. As he grows older, despite his extraordinary gift for storytelling, he realizes that he is always going to be an outcast. Drawn to the dark, seedy and dangerous underworld of Delhi, he turns his back on conventional society and makes himself at home with his new surrogate family comprising pimps, thugs, prostitutes and eunuchs (*hjiras*). In this community of outcasts he achieves fame and heroic status, but also the sense of worth and love he always longed for, to the point that he is no longer capable of distinguishing between imagination and reality; this leads ultimately to his downfall. Vamana is not for the faint-hearted or the conservative, as Adib Khan observes:

> Writing about odd characters is often an act of self-discovery. Conceiving a character like Vamana may also be a response to curiosity about a side of life a writer may know little about. It can be intimation that the imagination is tired and needs to be revived with the stimulant of something weird, something different. It can be an inadvertent process of shock learning that involves being up close and personal with people one would avoid. (2006, 2)

With the publication of *Homecoming* (2003), Khan displays "a fully Australian focus" (Matthews 2003, 52) through the central character of a Vietnam veteran, Martin Godwin, set in middle-class Australia, Melbourne and Daylesford, thus successfully replacing the presence of the subcontinent. Not surprisingly, the traumatic impact of the Vietnam War on Australian culture and thought has provided rich material for fiction. In response to the assumption of a monolithic communist threat and under US pressure, around 60,000 Australians served in Vietnam between 1962 and 1972 (Peel and Twomey 2011, 232), when Australian involvement ceased after it became clear that its strategy of forward defence was completely ineffective. Conscription for an unjust war was the primary issue for a peace movement that began with the lonely vigils of the women's group Save our Sons, and gradually grew into protests by radical students in the late 1960s and 1970s, developing into a counterculture expressing anti-authoritarian, anti-dominator and pro-partnership sentiments, reminiscent of the flourishing of a similar counterculture movement in the US that produced writers such as Jack Kerouac, Ken Kesey, Allen Ginsberg and Norman Mailer. In this turbulent period, literature and history appear deeply intertwined in novels such as Morris West's (1965) *The Ambassador*, and much later in Christopher Koch's (1995) *Highways to a War*, giving voice to a spirit of protest that went beyond the complexities of the Vietnam War itself and implied a blanket rejection of the restrictive suburban values of middle-aged Australia.[7] In poetry, Bruce Dawe's (1968) ironic elegy "Homecoming" directly expresses condemnation for the war where all warriors, American, Viet Cong, North Vietnamese, are "all victims, all vanquished" (13).

But Khan's *Homecoming* departs from this grim chapter of Australian history to quietly work for reconciliation, based on the human ability to look within and find "love, generosity and compassion" (228). Interestingly, Khan grew up in what was East Pakistan, another country ravaged by war, which became the independent nation of Bangladesh in 1971: his direct experience with the structural violence of his native country gave him a very different perspective on life and triggered a long period of soul-searching: "I made an effort to meet the real me by recording my reflections in fragmented bits of writing" (Khan 2003, 3). Although he turns away from writing about the subcontinent, the same tensions of displacement and belonging, a feature in all his novels, continue to acquire new depths and layers of meaning in *Homecoming*, which is concerned with the anxieties of Martin as his self-discovery gradually emerges to diffuse the painful brutality of his past and express a partnership consciousness through which he can truly connect with himself and the people around him.

Set in present-day Melbourne, the novel skilfully weaves together the multifaceted threads of Martin's life as a father, comrade, lover, unwilling conspirator and reluctant spiritual searcher. From the beginning of the story, shifting between flashbacks and the present, Martin is portrayed as a lonely man in his fifties, subsisting as a handyman and attending several university courses without completing any degree. His entire being is confused and burdened by the hideous memory of having fought "the loser's war" (Khan 2003, 68), tormented by nightmares "of agonised faces and burning landscapes, which stuck to him like viscous filth" (96). Like many who returned from that barbaric conflict, home is not the same any more and he finds himself like a migrant in his own land, living as a "fragment, exemplifying post-modernism" (135). As Martin admits, the killing and violence often did not last long, but "it's what happened afterwards. Much later. It's what you brought back with you. Memory – like an incurable disease" (186). The dominator configurations of warfare and killing, which retained such a grip on his life, find tangible reflections in his unsuccessful marriage, his difficult relationship with his son, his financial debts with the bank and his sexual impotence. As a soldier, Martin "was trained to achieve a state of controlled sanity in war" (129) in which "the display of emotion was a betrayal of toughness and the vigilant guardianship of a way of life" (37). In such a dominator system based on aggression, dominance and conquest, there is no place but for bullets: "they hum and sing, hurt and kill! That's the language we understand" (34). He has to live according to the strict dominator dichotomy of "it's either them or us […] no compromises. No in-betweens" (146), along with its inevitable barbaric behaviour, which culminates in the horrific episode of his comrades raping and shooting a young Vietnamese girl. This is the most traumatic event, which will haunt him for many years because, instead of intervening and preventing the rape, he turned and ran away in a cowardly fashion, thus evading "the kind of responsibility that defined the essence of humanity" (104). He has not been able to reveal this to his psychiatrist and it takes a long time to bring it out into the open, as "Vietnam is like an archaeological dig. The deeper you go, the more you unearth" (179). He will have to awaken from the "dominator trance"[8] and consciously unlearn the human capacity for destruction to relearn its inner partnership capacity for choice, empathy and love.

In this trajectory from alienation to connection, shifting from legacies of violence to a new-found sense of a shared humanity, Martin works "on issues that trouble him: loss, insanity, loneliness and despair" (Khan 2003, 41) with the caring and empathetic influence of three principal characters: his closest friend Colin, his partner Nora and his son's partner Maria. Colin, an intellectual who is dying of cancer, comforts Martin during and after the war through endless discussions around poetry and philosophy: "they have developed a trust, constancy and the certainty of mutual support where each is trying to make the most of the circumstances" (135). A particularly emblematic scene is one in which Colin is lecturing Martin on Plato's allegory of the cave through which their experience of disconnection is "similar to a prisoner exposed to the outside world" (223); what Martin and Colin have experienced has made them strangers to themselves and it is barely possible for those around them to understand what they have gone through. This is the unbearable strain that caused Martin's marriage to collapse, leaving him with "no strength of feeling inside him. Only the hollowness that echoed his shame of the war" (94).

His deep yearning to reinvent his past and re-imagine the future finds a new possibility of hope with Nora, "a slim brunette with infectious laughter" (Khan 2003, 69), who speaks gently to him and embraces his shortcomings, painful anxiety and sexual impotence with unconditional love. She knows that a lasting relationship is one "in which both people have learned to hide the cracks. Without accusation or blame" and Martin feels revived by her love "as the sheet he'd creased stretched flat under her hand" (95). However, within this unconventional relationship where they are "more than friends and less than partners" (116), Martin's self-transformation unfolds dramatically when Nora has a stroke, triggering a slow descent into insanity which will confine her to an institution. He continues to look after her finances and visit her, taking his turn to embrace her unconditionally; after all, as she unflinchingly demonstrates to him, "it's the entire person, flaws and all, that you learn to care about" (125).

This authentic expression of love and partnership is equally portrayed in the relationship between his son and Maria, where "the two have the strength of understanding each other, much more than words could give. It is the kind of awareness […] that's not based on any fixed idealism about relationships; they have the capacity to accommodate each other's weaknesses" (Khan 2003, 69). It is through Maria's honesty and her resilience in surmounting the consequences of war that Martin's quest for self-acceptance is further encouraged. As a Vietnamese Australian, Maria was deeply affected by the war, and also struggled initially to fit into Australian society, but it was through these struggles that she learnt never to hide who she was, thus overcoming in the process the dualism of her migrant identity. Maria embraces Martin as an intrinsic part of her life, encouraging him to connect deeply with both his son Frank, who suffers from depression, and Nora, whose irrational behaviour has set her apart from the world. Martin finds again the strength and courage to challenge and overcome his narrow-mindedness and inaction by unexpectedly visiting the yoga ashram frequented by his estranged son. Here, he entertains the possibility of untangling his problems by learning for the first time from a spiritual guide how fear and loneliness are used positively to develop self-growth. This is conveyed through the Buddhist tale of Kisagotami: a woman who loses her child and then learns through connecting with the universal suffering of others that no one is untouched by death. This story symbolically counteracts the disconnection highlighted in Plato's analogy of the cave, and after having left the ashram, Martin feels that he has been shown "a mesh of self-evaluation that was ultimately calming and fulfilling" (216). There is "a faint awareness of the beginnings of an alignment in his personality" (217) and he now feels ready "to clean up the mess and begin again" (230). He decides to share for the first time the rape episode with Colin, and this has a profound cathartic effect on them both, as they realize how separate their lives have been, and so reach a new-found intimacy. Colin admits that he has let himself down too by not speaking to him "about the fear of dying, or what it's like to be gay, and never to have had a partner […]. I, too, have hidden things that clutter the space inside" (231).

Martin is equally aware of how incapable he has been of speaking of love and experiencing intimacy in all his relationships: "an obsession with not indulging in self-pity and a quaint notion of manliness" has prevented him from being more "humanly vulnerable" (Khan 2003, 242). But he "knows that he is in the process of relinquishing the blighting effect of the war" (254) and can now see his future unfolding with clarity. He finds the courage to phone his local MP and speak out about the four soldiers who raped and shot the young Vietnamese girl. He then visits a Buddhist temple and lights a candle:

> the tapering light was like a two-way lens through which he could gaze into time, both the past and the future. Martin saw the girl, in the quietness of an afternoon, little more than a child. She smiled shyly and held up the friendly offering of vegetables to surly strangers. He thought of her as an adult, a mother, living the simple live of a villager. Then, in old age, she was a wise grandparent, sharing her experiences with a younger generation. And he saw masses of billowing smoke, giant plumes of fire, charred bodies and mangled people. (260)

From this new-found caring and mutual space, the dominator empathy-deadening violence of his difficult past is creatively reconfigured in his imagination and the partnership power to give, nurture and illuminate life is actualized. This pivotal disentanglement is further shown through the rekindling of his relationship with his son Frank and with Nora. After Frank's suicide attempt due to his depression, he and Martin truly connect with one another on a new and intimate level. As the novel draws to its close, Martin has found acceptance of life on its own flawed terms; he resolves to sell his old property, pay off his debts and bring Nora back to his new home in the countryside: "he thinks of the small house in front of the cluster of gum trees and the spaces around them like a vast canvas" (262), and for the first time since he has known Nora, he hears a note of pure joy in her laughter.

Khan further develops the complex issues relating to identity and belonging in *Spiral Road*, connecting these to the tragic events of the Pakistan/Bangladesh massacre in 1971 and the 9/11 Twin Towers attacks. The protagonist, Masud Alam, has lived in Australia for the past 30 years and reluctantly returns to Bangladesh to reconnect with his family. His father is succumbing to Alzheimer's disease, the family's wealth is gone and the city of his childhood no longer exists. His renewed contact with his home country and the Bangla language makes him feel "like a musician confronted with the tuning of an instrument that he hasn't played for years" (Khan 2007, 5). Like all Khan's characters, Masud is constantly struggling to renegotiate his relationship with the past "on the jagged edges of memory" (6) and re-imagining a more satisfying future beyond the dominator categories of "Us and Them. *For us or against us.* A complicated game, without rules" (267; emphasis in original). His inconspicuous life as a librarian in Melbourne is characterized by an unvarying routine where the unpredictable, chaotic and turbulent years of his past are stored in the recesses of his inner being. Home "is not a physical location any more. More like several places in the mind" (37) and "there will always be an awareness of the pieces that are missing. Now I'm unable to silence the voice of lament that whispers about denial and loss" (38). This sense of dislocation and not belonging also echoes in his relationship with Amelia, a widow living in Melbourne with her two teenaged daughters, to whom he is unable to make a commitment as his polarized self makes him feel like "an emotional Bedouin" (19) and "afraid of engaging intimately with anyone" (217). Not surprisingly, his unfixed identity does not neatly fit into national or religious categories: at the airport he is questioned for holding an Australian passport and for not being a practising Muslim, yet ironically welcomed as a war hero as soon as officials come to know that he was a freedom fighter in the liberation war against Pakistan:

> I've never thought that I was a kind of a hero. But then people have funny notions about valour. Once I was among those classified as freedom fighters. *Terrorist* to some … *insurgent* to other. Miscreant to the Pakistani soldiers. I was nicknamed Explosive and even made it to the top ten on the army's MOST WANTED list. (27; emphasis in original)

His extended family has a rich cultural background linked to the wealthy and influential *zamindari* (landowners) tradition, where family honour (*izzat*), a feudalistic hierarchical structure and loyalty to the Qur'an are unquestionable marks of the Islamic way of life. Masud was instead brought up under the influence of both Christianity and Islam, and as a "lapsed Muslim" (19) is reluctant to abide by any religion: "unquestioning submission to an omnipotent God is beyond my capability. I wish I had the gift of religious faith. Sometimes I long to believe in a structured universe designed purposefully for mankind" (89).

With his provisional and shifting sense of identity, Masud is gradually brought face to face with the cultural Manichean insularity of both Bangladesh and Australia; he is confronted by conservative family members like Uncle Rafiq who disparagingly sees the 9/11 attack as a successful retaliation against the west's veneer of arrogance; by Steven Mills and Peter Nicholas, Australian and American secret service agents, who suspect him of being a terrorist; and by a group of religious zealots who threateningly surround him demanding he recite a chapter of the Qur'an (*surah*) to prove he is Muslim. However, these dominator world views are equally interpolated by partnership configurations, such as those professed by Alya, who challenges conservative mullahs by empowering country women in her factory where they can find collective strength against the feudal system still in place in some rural villages; Nasreen, who finds the courage to walk away from her violent and abusive husband; and Masud's father, Abba, who abandoned a life of luxury to pursue medicine, a choice which went against family values as "anyone who has to work every day to make a living is an insult to *zamindars*" (32).

Khan gradually weaves terrorism into a story of family secrets which challenge the traditional value of family loyalty and Masud's sense of identity. He first discovers a previous extra-conjugal relationship of his father's by examining old family papers, and this compels him to perceive his father as an equal:

> Is it possible to reinvent your own father? Slash the image that you've carried for so long? Bruise and cut him, make him bleed and then stand back, like a painter surveying a picture he has just completed, and say: "There! He is now human." (Khan 2007, 285)

This is a turning point in Masud's life in which the possibility of renegotiating his past and embracing a more empathetic future unfolds: "ours was the sin of turning him into a demigod, someone we assumed was without flesh and desire, without instinct or temptation" (359). He finds consolation in discovering his father's weaknesses and realizes how many corrections and adjustments his parents' long relationship has required, thus making him feel like "an emotional simpleton, my limitations cruelly exposed" (218). This prompts him impulsively to call Amelia to let her know how much he cares. He is now more at ease with his fissured self and flaws, and this makes him feel more authentically human: "perhaps wisdom is in seeing our own failures, how we misdirected our energies? Nothing is entirely pure or sacred or certain as we grow older. Nowadays my dreams are rarely grand or fresh. They're smudged and chipped" (263).

This shift in consciousness paves the way for the unravelling of a more disturbing family secret: his beloved nephew, Omar, who returned to Dhaka from Seattle after 9/11 to allegedly set up his own textile business, is a jihadist determined to establish a domestic terrorist cell amongst tribal people in the rural hill regions. Omar's descent into the orbit of terrorism has been triggered by the harassment and alienation he experienced soon after 9/11. Although as horrified as everyone else, he finds himself caught up in the sweeping generalizations of revenge for being a Muslim. He is handcuffed and bundled off to prison, interrogated and beaten by police: "the 'rightness' of inequality. You're intended to feel inferior" (Khan 2007, 288). Out of despair, he regains his dignity and finds a sense of purpose by joining a terrorist network where "victim becomes aggressor in the vengeful and ever widening cycle of a life for a life. Spiral Road" (292).

Significantly, the novel departs from the usual cultural divide stimulated by simplistic political rhetoric – what Mamdami (2002) terms "Culture Talk" (766) – that sees both Islam and the west as irredeemably different, to show that the real "clash of civilizations" takes place fundamentally within the common ground of the human heart, where the impetus to dominate others is fuelled by "a monopoly on righteousness and truth" (Khan 2007, 302) at the cost of human life. This is powerfully conveyed through the telling of Masud's involvement in the Bangladesh war of 1971, another dominator ramification where "Muslims in the East were tainted by Hindu culture" (226). During this period, when the resistance was gathering momentum, Masud recollects a guerrilla fight against an army patrol in which, in a moment of panic, he opened fire, causing a crossfire in which innocent Bengali civilians lost their lives. At that time, he did not know "about the enemies who come back inside every fighter. Those invisible forces that slowly disassemble you" (88) and this traumatic experience shatters his idealistic ambitions for freedom, causing him intense pain and guilt:

> Headlines screamed of atrocities, treachery and the callousness of miscreants and traitors. Us. There was no mention of an army patrol. The gruesome photographs of children's bodies scattered on the ground culminated the propaganda triumph for the Pakistani army. (124–125)

By recalling the many atrocities perpetrated during the nine-month Bangladesh war for independence, Khan revisits the myths surrounding the Independence War and the forging of the country's national identity, through which Masud comes to painfully understand that "you can create illusions of nobility and great deeds, and hide behind them. But recollections and the guilt resurface later. You feel stained and dirty" (121). Having directly experienced the insidiousness of war, "the way it can slowly wreck those who return, even as heroes" (191), he has been able to transcend the dominator continuum of violence by realizing that no one can win in this struggle "but the foolishness of what you're doing to yourself" (307). He has seen the errors of his ways, "soul-mangling errors that crippled you permanently. They suck out the marrow of life and leave you like the drought-stricken bed of a pond. A cracked and parched surface littered with the memories of what you once were" (122). Having gained deep insights into the futility of war – "I realised how broken up I was inside" (308) – he feels compelled to free Omar from the same disillusionment by communicating to him as an equal and empathetically talking "about flaws, treachery and lies. Hurt and healing. Fallibilities in a genuine relationship […]. Closeness is about shared imperfections. One may admire saints, but I doubt if you can have intimate relationships with them" (310). This, however, only reinforces Omar's allegiance to the dominator view of a world divided into in-groups and out-groups, with those who are different seen as enemies to be conquered or destroyed: whereas he is totally committed to ending "global dominance by white nations […] and restoring Muslim dignity" (300). Masud leaves him with the firm belief that "nothing is worth the loss of lives!" (191). Unfortunately, at the end of the novel, both Omar and Masud's journeys dramatically come full circle: Omar is shot and killed protecting Masud who was targeted at the airport whilst escaping. Masud then decides to remain in Bangladesh, "unable to run any more" (362).

To conclude, both *Homecoming* and *Spiral Road* explore the same tensions of displacement and belonging by embracing humanity and its flaws through Martin's and Masud's restless quest for self-knowledge. Through the process of constant renegotiation and reinterpretion of the past, the official dominator ideals of orthodox values, institutionalized violence and cultural stereotypes are transcended and stripped away, thus allowing the protagonists to celebrate the vitality of imperfection and reveal their humanness. I would argue that these very tensions animate all Khan's central characters: in fact, Iqbal in *Seasonal Adjustment* is seen as overcoming dominator binarisms by realizing that "behind the trappings of cultural differences human strengths and failures are global constants" (Khan 1994, 143). Khalid, in *Solitude of Illusions*, having chosen a life of mediocrity, perceives the limitations and burdens he has created by living according to his oppressive family's obligations; Vamana, in *The Storyteller*, whose inclusive worlds exude the odour of humanity, exposes the real flawed humanness characterized by corrupt politicians, unhappy marriages and hypocritical priests. Similarly, Martin and Masud progress from alienation to connection, overcoming the blighting effects of war to reach a new found sense of a shared humanity, beyond violence and other forms of inequality and oppression. Khan's iconic protagonists all defiantly exhibit the limitations of rigidly defined identities and national boundaries, monologic ideologies and the imperfections of moral acceptability, where " 'RIGHT' and 'WRONG' are woefully inadequate words to describe the greyness of the world" (Khan 2007, 229) they traverse. From this rejection of the binarism of "either/or" and "us/them", far from being merely fictional, they are very much more functional, enabling the author to imaginatively rehearse complex issues around his yearnings for connection and belonging, in which memory and imagination work dynamically: "what memory cannot provide, the imagination does. The liaison between 'fact' and 'fiction' is sandpapered by the artistic craft to produce a seamless product" (Khan 2015, 12). Arguably, as Eisler's partnership/ dominator models highlight, the epistemological violence of dominator systems with its asymmetrical binary relationships is effectively transcended when diversity – be it based on gender, religion or ethnic origin – is no longer equated with either superiority or inferiority but valued as enriching the ways for recreating in dialogic and relational terms a new empathetic future.

Notes

1. Khan's first novel *Seasonal Adjustments* (1994) won the Christina Stead Prize for Fiction, the Book of the Year award in the 1994 New South Wales Premier's Literary Awards and the 1995 Commonwealth Writers' Prize for Best Book, and was also shortlisted for the 1994 Age Book of the Year award. *Solitude of Illusions* (1996) was shortlisted for the Christina Stead Prize for Fiction, and the Ethnic Affairs Commission Award, and won the 1997 Tilly Aston Braille Book of the Year Award.
2. Abdulla's stories started appearing in periodicals such as the *Bulletin*, *Quadrant* and *Hemisphere* in 1953 and were subsequently published in book form as *The Time of the Peacock*, jointly authored by Abdullah and Mathew (1965).
3. For a detailed discussion of the partnership model in world literatures, languages and education, see the publications listed in official website of the Partnership Studies Group (PSG), http://all.uniud.it/?page_id=198.
4. "'Equalitarian' is used instead of the more conventional 'egalitarian' which traditionally has only described equality between men and men (as the works of Locke, Rousseau, and other 'rights of man' philosophers, as well as modern history, evidence). 'Equalitarian' denotes social relations in a partnership society where women and men (and 'masculine' and 'feminine') are accorded equal value" (Eisler 1987, 216).
5. Eisler distinguishes "between *domination hierarchies* characterized by a predominantly authoritarian social structure ultimately backed by force or fear of pain, which inhibit the actualization of both oneself and others' highest potentials, and *actualization hierarchies* in which power is used to empower rather than disempower others" (Mercanti 2014, 17; emphases in original).
6. For a detailed analysis of the novel, see Mercanti (2012).
7. Another significant expression of protest is the anthology of prose and verse edited by Shirley Cass, Ros Cheney, David Malouf and Michael Wilding (1971), *We Took Their Orders and Are Dead*.
8. The legitimization of violence as the only real and cosmically grounded reality, a dominator way of thinking and living within a system in which the human need for caring connection is associated with either the infliction or suffering of pain. Hence, pain, abuse and injustice are repressed in one's unconscious mind and, as required to maintain a domination system, legitimized as the way things are supposed to be (see Eisler 1987, 1995, 2014).

Disclosure statement

No potential conflict of interest was reported by the author.

References

Abdullah, Mena, and Ray Mathew. 1965. *The Time of the Peacock*. Sydney: Angus and Robertson.
Cass, Shirley, Ros Cheney, David Malouf, and Michael Wilding, eds. 1971. *We Took Their Orders and are Dead: An Anti-War Anthology*. Sydney: Ure Smith.

Dawe, Bruce. 1968. "Review of *Homecoming*." *The Age*, 6 July: 13.

Eisler, Riane. 1987. *The Chalice and the Blade: Our History, Our Future*. San Francisco, CA: Harper and Row.

Eisler, Riane. 1995. *Sacred Pleasure: Sex, Myth and the Politics of the Body*. San Francisco, CA: Harper Collins.

Eisler, Riane. 2014. "Human Possibilities: The Interaction of Biology and Culture." *Interdisciplinary Journal of Partnership Studies* 1 (1): 1–38.

Greet, Anne. 2000. "Angels and Demons (Review of *The Storyteller*)." *The Age* 9 September: 11.

Helff, Sissy. 2009. "Multicultural Australia and Transcultural Unreliable Narration in Indian-Australian Literature." In *Bernard Hickey, a Roving Cultural Ambassador: Essays in his Memory*, edited by Maria Renata Dolce, and Antonella Riem Natale, 135–147. Udine: Forum.

Jose, Nicholas. 2015. *Everyday and Exotic: Australian Asian Writing*. Melbourne: The Wheeler Centre. http://www.wheelercentre.com/projects/the-long-view/everyday-and-exotic-australian-asian-writing.

Khan, Adib. 1994. *Seasonal Adjustments*. Sydney: Allen and Unwin.

Khan, Adib. 1996. *Solitude of Illusions*. Sydney: Allen and Unwin.

Khan, Adib. 2000. "Trends in Australian Fiction." In *Kosmopolis*, 1–9. Barcelona: Centre de Cultura Contemporània de Barcelona, CCCB.

Khan, Adib. 2003. *Homecoming*. Pymble, NSW: Flamingo.

Khan, Adib. 2006. "Cruising: A Writer's Journey." *The Daily Star* 5 (793): 1–4.

Khan, Adib. 2007. *Spiral Road*. Sydney: Harper Collins.

Khan, Adib. 2013. "Here, There." In *Joyful Strains. Making Australia Home*, edited by Kent MacCarter, and Ali Lemer, 189–200. Melbourne: Affirm Press.

Khan, Adib. 2015. "Diasporic Homes." *Le Simplegadi* 13 (14): 8–14.

Kirkpatrick, Peter, and Robert Dixon, eds. 2012. *Republics of Letters: Literary Communities in Australia*. Sydney: Sydney University Press.

Koch, Christopher. 1995. *Highways to a War*. Melbourne: Heinemann.

Mamdami, Mahmood. 2002. "Good Muslim, Bad Muslim: A Political Perspective on Culture and Terrorism." *American Anthropologist* 104 (3): 766–775.

Matthews, David. 2003. "Anything Goes: Review of *Homecoming* by Adib Khan." *Australian Book Review* 256: 52.

Mercanti, Stefano. 2012. "'No Better or Worse Than Anyone, But an Equal': Negotiating Mutuality in Adib Khan's *Seasonal Adjustments*." *Journal of the Association for the Study of Australian Literature (JASAL)* 12 (2): 1–13.

Mercanti, Stefano. 2014. "Glossary for Cultural Transformation: The Language of Partnership and Domination." *Interdisciplinary Journal of Partnership Studies (IJPS)* 1 (1): 1–36. http://pubs.lib.umn.edu/ijps/vol1/iss1/4/.

National English Curriculum, Draft Consultation version 1.1.0. 2011. *Australian Curriculum*. Assessment and Report Authority (ACARA). http://www.australiancurriculum.edu.au/Static/docs/history/3.0/Australian%20Curriculum%20v2.0.pdf.

Ommundsen, Wenche. 2012. "Transnational Imaginaries: Reading Asian Australian Writing. Introduction." *Journal of the Association for the Study of Australian Literature* 12 (2): 1–8.

Peel, Mark, and Christina Twomey. 2011. *A History of Australia*. Basingstoke: Palgrave Macmillan.

Riem, Antonella Natale. 2015. "Partnership Studies: A New Methodological Approach to Literary Criticism in World Literatures, Languages and Education." *Interdisciplinary Journal of Partnership Studies (IJPS)* 2 (1): 1–9. http://pubs.lib.umn.edu/ijps/vol2/iss1/3/.

Sarwal, Amit. 2015. *Labels and Locations: Gender, Family, Class and Cast: The Short Narratives of South Asian Diaspora in Australia*. Newcastle upon Tyne: Cambridge Scholars Publishing.

West, Morris. 1965. *The Ambassador*. London: Heinemann.

Index

Page numbers with "n" refer to endnotes.

www.ingramcontent.com/pod-product-compliance
Ingram Content Group UK Ltd.
Pitfield, Milton Keynes, MK11 3LW, UK
UKHW010021280225
455677UK00023B/730